# CONTENTS

# CHAPTER ONE

# HORSES FOR COURSES?

'Horses for courses' is such a cliché that even people who have not the slightest interest in racing know what it means and use it to describe patterns of behaviour quite unrelated to racing. But how *true* is it? Does it apply to all kinds of races, or only to certain kinds of races?

The second question is easier to answer. With some kinds of races, it is simply impossible to decide whether the cliché is true, because there are not enough of these races to enable you to make a statistical analysis of the results. To prove this point, I will look at different kinds of races in turn.

In non-handicap races, what makes the Classic races so fascinating to all journalists and many racegoers is that there is hardly any previous form over course and distance. For the Derby and Oaks runners, there are no previous races over course and distance. Therefore, instead of a balanced discussion of relevant form, the reams of newspaper comment fall into three categories: endless discussions of trial races over courses which are mostly nothing like Epsom, including races which have been run *in the previous season*; agonising over breeding; and, this is my particular favourite, falling back on the perceptive-sounding comment that 'X's style of racing suggests that he will get further.'

The Newmarket Classics have more in their favour, in that there are a handful of races over the distance, which can more justifiably be regarded as pointers to Classic success. On the other hand, these races may have been run in the previous season, and it is well known that two-year-olds often fail to train on in their second season.

What is true of the Classics, is also true of most Group and Listed races. Look through the programme of these races run at the leading courses, such as Doncaster, Goodwood, Newmarket, Sandown, and York, and you will see that there are very few races run over the same course and distance. In these non-handicap races, a winner at a given course and distance has to step up in class the next time, and it is very difficult to weigh up the effect of even a minor rise in class e.g. from a Group 3 to a Group 2.

When assessing some of the big handicaps, you are faced with a similar difficulty. The Cambridgeshire is the only 1m 1f handicap at the Newmarket Rowley mile course during the season; likewise, the Cesarewitch is the only 2m 2f race at the same course. There are no previous course and distance races in the same season for the 6f Wokingham, the 1m Royal Hunt Cup, or the 5f 140y Portland Handicap. There are 'Key Races' for some of these races but, although very reliable, the right combination does not occur every season.

It is only in run-of-the-mill handicap racing that there are enough course and distance races to make it possible to decide whether 'horses for courses' is statistically justified. Take a month early in the season, May, from what was a representative season, 1995, and analyse the handicaps at all distances run over the following courses:

Ascot
Bath
Beverley
Catterick
Doncaster
Goodwood
Newcastle

# How to Beat the Handicapper

Newmarket
Pontefract
Ripon
Thirsk
Warwick
Windsor

In May 1995, 63 handicaps were staged at these courses, and in 27 of these there was at least one course and distance winner, i.e. 43% of the races. Later on in the season, when there is much more form in the book, the position is even better: there are many more handicaps; and a higher proportion of these feature at least one course and distance winner.

Thus in July, 1995, there were 104 races in handicaps over all distances at the above courses; and of these, 58 (56%) included at least one course and distance winner. Throughout the season as a whole, at the courses listed above, there were at least 200 races in which there was a course and distance winner. 1995 was not an exceptional season, and a similar overall total and distribution pattern of course and distance winners occur year after year. This means that over a period of ten years, there are around 2,000 races for analysis.

With such a large number of course and distance winners of handicap races, you can start looking for patterns and trends, so as to be able to identify those courses which are particularly favourable to course and distance winners, in a way which is simply not possible with other types of races.

The only way to settle the question of which courses do favour specialists given the current programme of racing is by analysing results over a period of time. This book is based on analysis of ten seasons' results (1985-94). I consider that a course and distance can be regarded as suitable for specialists if, during this period, there have been at least 10 possible selections, involving 10 different horses; and if, overall, selections have shown a 50% winning strike-rate. It is important that there should be at least 10 different horses, rather than 10 selections, as otherwise a handful of horses which record multiple wins might give a distorted picture.

Given that so much data is available, it is surprising that there are systems compilers who have gone to great lengths to try and find equivalencies between different courses. For example, it is sometimes argued that you can make an equivalence between different courses on the similarity of their standard times. On this basis, the Folkestone 5f course would be 'equivalent' to the Newmarket 5f Rowley Mile course, since the standard time for the former is 58.6 seconds, and for the latter, 58.7 seconds. One is flat, the other is undulating - yet on the basis of the time theory, they would be 'equivalent'.

Furthermore, in this system, it is impossible to see how you can isolate the different class of runners at Folkestone and Newmarket as a separate variable. Better class horses running on a more testing course would give the same standard time as poorer class horses running on a much easier course.

Even if you could make this equivalence, it seems an unnecessarily complicated process when there is so much straightforward, comparing like-with-like course and distance form available over a long period of time.

To continue with the argument. Of course, the selections are not made by backing every course and distance winner without further thought. Before beginning the analysis, I had in mind a few common-sense rules which would exclude certain qualifiers (e.g. had not won for a considerable period of time; had not won on the going).

These rules are to be found in chapter 3. When tested over a ten-year period, they were found to exclude a large proportion of the losers, leaving an overall strike-rate of

50%. This is an average - some courses fall significantly below the average, and are consequently excluded and others are either average or above average. In most seasons, the strike-rate does not rise greatly above, or fall significantly below the average. For example, in the season analysed in chapter 5, the strike-rate was 53%, slightly, but not significantly, above average.

In some cases, the results show that a course must definitely be discounted as a specialists' course because the strike-rate of course and distance qualifiers is too low. In others, there are not enough analysed results to enable you to make a judgement - the programme of handicap racing as currently organised simply does not offer the course and distance specialist enough opportunities.

There is also one distance which, in the long term, gives more favourable results than any other. I emphasise in the long term, because if you looked at the 1995 results and saw that there were five losers out of five selections over this distance, you might be rather sceptical. Seven furlongs is a specialists' distance because it demands too much stamina of the sprinter, and too much speed of the mile runner.

There are very few courses which offer a testing straight seven furlongs, either flat or uphill. This is where the organisation of the racing programme becomes so crucial. For example, Newbury has two seven-furlong courses, one round, the other straight. In the current programme, there are five races at the former and only two over the latter. If the numbers were reversed, I feel confident that there would be more course specialists. Remember that the programme does change. For example, since 1990 at Redcar there has been a significant increase in the number of races over 7f.

Where the programme is suitably organised, 7f races offer some of the certainties of the season. The Newmarket 7f races are the prime example, and 1995 was very much the exception (one loser, CADEAUX TRYST, Race 2948 5 August). (n.b. All race numbers are those of the official British Horseracing Board record, as given in *Raceform* and *Raceform Update*). In previous seasons the record was exemplary (PERFOLIA 1991; HOB GREEN 1992; EN ATTENDANT 1993 and 1994; and POLISH ADMIRAL 1994).

The reader who is still not convinced may be wondering how to check my analysis, and whether to do so requires the use of a computer. Let me assure you that a computer is quite unnecessary for this purpose. I do not have any programming skills, and could not have begun to use the computer to analyse results.

In any case, a computer friend assured me that the time required to programme a computer to analyse races in the way I do (see chapter 3 for a full explanation) and, more importantly, the time required to enter the data, would far exceed that spent in using pen and paper, and recording the results on index cards.

I use a computer only to collate and store my analysis and results. This is in no way necessary, and you could make do equally well with a an indexed notebook.

In chapter 2, I sort racecourses into three distinct categories: courses definitely suited to specialists; courses definitely not suited; and those for which there is not enough evidence (and why). To anticipate the findings set out in that chapter:

Of the 34 Flat racecourses in Britain,

9 are specialists courses at all distances
9 are specialists courses at some distances
3 are definitely not suited to course and distance winners
13 are impossible to assess.

Therefore, almost half of the Flat racecourses in Britain are definitely not suited to course and distance winners, or are impossible to assess.

In Ireland, because of its much more restricted programme of Flat racing, it is only possible to assess four out of the 25 courses, but all these four turn out to favour course and distance winners.

Unlike every other racing cliché bar one ('a horse can give away weight but not distance' - see chapter 4, under 'Can reverse the form'), 'horses for courses' is perfectly true, when limited to certain courses.

Specialisation as to course and distance can go even further. In handicap racing, there are also a surprising number of horses which have not only won over the same course and distance, but which have also won the same race, either in the previous season or the season before that. Consider the following two examples, both from 1995.

LORD HIGH ADMIRAL won a 5f handicap at Haydock on 28 May 1994 (Race 1224) by three-quarters of a length, ridden out. By the time the same race came round again in 1995, he had run eight more races (five in 1994, three in 1995) without winning. His three previous races in 1995 were not very promising: twelfth on his seasonal debut (Race 693 Newbury 5f 34y); third in a five-runner claimer (Race 944 8 May Doncaster 5f); and thirteenth (Race 1106 17 May York 5f handicap). The Handicapper had taken notice of these rather feeble performances, and reduced his mark to 1lb lower than that of his 1994 win. Carrying 1lb in weight more than in 1994, LORD HIGH ADMIRAL showed his appreciation by winning the same race again, this time more comfortably, by two and a half lengths (Race 1304 27 May).

Remember that the crucial figure is the mark, not the weight. In this case the distinction does not matter, as there was not a significant discrepancy between the handicap mark and the weight carried. In 1994, LORD HIGH ADMIRAL won off 87, carrying 9st 13lb; in the same race in the following season, he was rated 86, and carried 10st. Only in the exceptional cases, where the weights have been raised considerably because of the defection of the horses initially allocated the top weight, would there be a marked discrepancy between the mark and the weight. Then you would have to be confident that the horse concerned had shown himself able to carry heavier weights.

In an even more striking example of a repeat version of the same race (Race 934 7 May 1995 Newmarket 6f), MASTER PLANNER won the same race off the same handicap mark by the same winning margin. When he won a Newmarket 6f handicap at the end of April 1994 (Race 743), the five-year-old MASTER PLANNER was rated 96, the highest mark from which he had ever won a race. The Handicapper seemed to re-assess him rather harshly for a game half-length win, by increasing his mark to 101, i.e. as if he had won by just under two lengths. Events showed that at above a rating of 96, MASTER PLANNER was firmly in the grip of the Handicapper, as he failed to win any of his twelve subsequent races in 1994. He continued to run honestly, but his best effort was being beaten by four lengths into third place in a competitive sprint handicap at the York August meeting (Race 3254 31 August 1994). By the end of the season, his rating was still 2lb above that of his solitary win - if horses could speak to the Handicapper, MASTER PLANNER would surely have said: 'Give me a break, will you!'

In the close-season, the Handicapper reviews all the handicap marks, and frequently relaxes his grip on horses which have won only one race early in the past season. MASTER PLANNER was a beneficiary of the season of good will, and in his first race of the 1995 season, found that he had returned to a mark of 96, while carrying 3lb more. He celebrated by winning more comfortably than on the previous occasion, so that the Handicapper raised his mark to 102. By the end of the season, he had lost all ten of his races, and his mark was down to 94.

In handicaps, this specialisation can go even further. A horse may win the same race three times in succession (AMRON won the 5f handicap at Doncaster at the first meeting of the season in 1991, 1992, and 1993). Admittedly, this is rather exceptional, but there are several instances of a horse winning the same race two or even three

# How to Beat the Handicapper

years later (the most recent examples being AMBUSCADE Race 3797 3 October 1994 Pontefract; CASTLEREA LAD Race 1241 24 May 1995 Goodwood; KALAR Race 3357 25 August 1995 Thirsk).

Very occasionally, this gives you an opportunity to consider a horse which has won one of the big handicaps over unusual distances (e.g. DAWN'S DELIGHT, Portland Handicap 1984 and 1987; BARONET, the Cambridgeshire 1978 and 1980; RAMBO'S HALL, the Cambridgeshire 1989 and 1992).

These are striking results, and the reader may be as incredulous as I was when I first looked at same race winners. He may object: surely these are just coincidences? surely there can not be enough of these races to identify any patterns or trends?

The answer is as surprising as the results. It is that although there are relatively few such races each season, over a longer period (say, ten seasons) there are enough cases to make it possible to search for patterns. In an average season, there are usually around 15 handicap races contested by the winner of the same race in the previous season. Not many, especially given that this represents less than 1% of a season's handicap races, but over a ten-year period, it adds up to at least 150 races.

An analysis of these races shows that, only in this case, the winning style is quite immaterial. A horse which has been all out to win a race has a good chance of winning the same race again provided that it is running off the same or a lower mark.

It also shows that, once the season gets into gear (from the Epsom Derby meeting at the beginning of June), there are fewer instances of same race winners trying for a repeat version and even these have too low a strike-rate to make them worth backing. It seems reasonable to suppose that these horses run well early in the season when fresh, but not so well thereafter.

The rules for backing same race winners, therefore, are:

1. before the beginning of June, if they have not won this season, they must be on the same or a lower mark than when winning the same race in the previous season.

2. before the beginning of June, the winning style of their previous season's race is immaterial.

3. from the beginning of June, they must have won a race in acceptable style during the current season.

These conditions may seem very restrictive, but in 1995, a typical season, they produced the following selections:

| Race | 535 | 5 April | PALACEGATE TOUCH | W 9-1 |
|------|------|---------|-------------------|--------|
| Race | 934 | 7 May | MASTER PLANNER | W 9-1 |
| Race | 1036 | 12 May | ROLLING THE BONES | W 11-10 |
| Race | 1106 | 17 May | SADDLEHOME | L 7-1 |
| Race | 1179 | 20 May | HI NOD | L 6-1 |
| Race | 1202 | 22 May | VANBOROUGH LAD | W 8-1 |
| Race | 1268 | 25 May | GOOD HAND | W 4-1 |
| Race | 1344 | 29 May | MIDNIGHT JAZZ | L 8-1 |
| Race | 1513 | 5 June | SCENIC DANCER | L 7-2 |

Given such striking results - 9 selections, and a 55% strike-rate - it is worth asking two questions: why do same race winners occur so frequently in handicaps? why do same race winners not occur so frequently in non-handicaps?

The first question is easily answered. Eventually, the Handicapper has no choice but to reduce a horse's rating following several losing runs over the 'wrong' course. This works very much in the favour of the horse which tends to win only when fresh - the rest of the season is spent 'running off' the mark. I am not suggesting any dubious practice on the part of the trainer since, with this type of horse, there really is no alternative. Such horses just feel 'right' at a particular part of the season, and repeat their best performances.

The answer to the second lies in the structure of the racing programme. There are some non-handicap races which are won again by the same horse. An outstanding example is FURTHER FLIGHT, who in 1995 won the Jockey Club Cup Stakes (Race 3946 30 September Newmarket 2m) for the fifth consecutive time. But there are very few of these races in the programme; and the fact that all these races are at level weights (with the exception of weight-for-age allowances, and small penalties for previous victories) means that the handicap 'check' of being above or below the previous limit rating does not operate. It is then, literally speaking, very difficult to weigh up such races.

An analysis of course and distance winners disproves a well-worn racing cliché, that 'horses are not machines'. They are not the kind of machines which operate to tolerances of a millionth of an inch, under all kinds of circumstances; but they are not very different from machines which operate at more generous tolerances, given certain conditions. You would not expect a mechanically operated clock to operate under water, or in a desert; and even under normal conditions, you would allow for it to gain a few seconds a day.

Given similar conditions, a high proportion of horses do turn in remarkably similar performances, as the record of same race winners shows. Of courses, horses do have their 'off' days when they run accountably badly, but these are not so frequent as is supposed. Certainly they are not enough to give real substance to the cliché, although they are enough to offer lazy journalists an excuse for their failure to analyse races thoroughly.

It is also worth understanding why a system focused on course and distance winners gives such excellent results, because you would then be able to understand and anticipate why it might stop working.

The most important reason is that British and Irish Flat racing still takes place on a wide variety of courses - uphill, downhill, almost circular, oval, figure of eight - unequalled in the world. The three All-Weather racecourses (Lingfield, Southwell, and Wolverhampton) are much more uniform in character, which may explain why the results to date are disappointing.

It is this variety of course types which gives the backer a competitive edge against the Handicapper. If a horse wins reasonably well over a given course and distance, the Handicapper may be able to take his measure over that course and distance. But if the winner runs two or three times over quite a different course, or distance, the Handicapper has no option but to reduce the mark. Here the course and distance winner has a dual advantage: his course expertise is underrated by his mark; while his opponents' difficulties in handling the course are overrated by their marks.

Whatever he may privately think about the desirability of doing so, the Handicapper can not produce two sets of marks - one of which is for a given course and distance. I only hope that this does not give the Official Handicapper food for thought!

The course and distance advantage has always been a part of British and Irish racing. In some ways the backer has fewer opportunities today than a generation ago, with the disappearance of courses such as Alexandra Park. But on balance the current programme of racing favours the course and distance winner to a greater extent than ever before - for three reasons.

Firstly, the great expansion in the number of race meetings over the last twenty years has meant a correspondingly great increase in the number of races run over the same course and distance.

Secondly, a change in the pattern of ownership and methods of training. A much higher proportion and number of horses are owned by partnerships. The idea of keeping a horse under wraps for the one great *coup* does not greatly appeal to a syndicate of owners, because they want to see their horse running as often as possible. Given the high quality of the bookmakers' intelligence network, it would also be very difficult to organise a successful *coup* if a syndicate of ten or more owners was involved.

Finally, methods of training have also changed, to a great extent in response to the demands of partnerships. Following the lead of Martin Pipe, trainers get their horses much fitter on the home gallops and race them much more frequently. On the Flat, Mark Johnston, a very capable trainer, is one of many who uses this method. A typical horse of this kind is STAR RAGE. Even though he races over the longer distances (around two miles), he ran twenty seven times in 1994 (including two on the All-Weather), and seventeen times in 1995. In the not too distant past, it was only sprint handicappers who had to undergo such a punishing schedule. It does mean that such horses will run more often over a suitable course and distance than they would have done a few years ago.

The remainder of the book is structured as follows: chapters 2 and 3 set out the process of arriving at a selection; chapter 4 tells you when to bet; and chapter 5 shows the system in action, in 1995.

# CHAPTER TWO

# COURSES FOR HORSES

This chapter begins the process of arriving at a selection. Every racing day you should follow a set routine, in which the first step is: are there any course and distance races which should be looked at? Such is the fullness of the modern racing programme that in 1995 there were only ten days on which there were no qualifying races. But on many more days than that (usually at least fifty per season, just under one third), a glance at the paper will show that there are no course and distance qualifiers to consider, so you can save your energy for another day.

Before discussing which courses are suitable for this system, I must emphasise again that you can only identify these courses by analysing the results. You can not tell simply by looking at the conformation of the course that it favours specialists. For example, a first glance at Brighton and Chester shows that they are very peculiar courses indeed - the former, with its switch-back conformation, the latter with its tight, circular layout. At Chester, the strike-rate is too low; whereas at Brighton, the racing programme does not generate enough cases from which to draw any conclusions.

At some courses, it seems probable that there would be course specialists, but the organisation of the racing programme does not give them enough opportunities. For example, at Ascot there are only two 7f all-aged handicaps: one at the first meeting (end of April), the other at the penultimate meeting (end of September). Winners of the first handicap so rarely contest the second that it is not possible to decide whether this is a specialists' distance.

The structure of the handicap programme is particularly important in Ireland, where the overwhelming majority of courses have either only one or two meetings per season, or these meetings are spaced at rather lengthy intervals. The exceptions are the two Dublin courses, Leopardstown and The Curragh, which have a regular programme of racing throughout the season; and the Festival courses, Galway and Tralee, which also have enough racing to enable us to form a judgement. Because of this, only these courses are discussed below.

Yet, as changes in the last four years or so have shown, the racing programme is not immutable. At the moment, it seems that it will include more racing, not less, which is very much in favour of the course and distance specialist. It is worth keeping up your records of untested course and distance races, to take advantage of any changes which may occur. For example, from 1990, the series of races at Redcar over 7f is ideally timed to suit a specialist, and within a year or two enough examples should be available to judge whether this is a specialists' course.

I now give my findings for every racecourse in Britain, and the four exceptional courses in Ireland. Below each course, I have listed the selections for 1995, not only so that you can easily check the results against your own analysis, but also as a useful reference guide for the future.

For ease of reference, a list of all the suitable courses and distances is given at the end of this chapter.

## BRITISH COURSES

### ASCOT
The Royal Hunt Cup Mile, most of which is uphill, is a very demanding course, and the round course is equally testing. The paradox is that, although Ascot form is very reliable at other courses, this does not mean that Ascot itself is a specialists' course.

# How to Beat the Handicapper

Here is a prime example of a course which offers few opportunities to the course and distance specialist because of the way in which the current racing programme is organised. For other reasons (see below), this is an unrewarding course for my system.

5f: at this distance there are currently four races per season, in June, July, September and October, just enough to make an analysis possible. However, although there have been repeat course and distance winners here (the most recent being SPANIARDS CLOSE, in 1995), there have not been enough selections to justify saying that this is a specialist course and distance.

If you do decide to apply the system here, remember that, even excluding horses which have not won on the prevailing going, winners of the (0-110) handicap at the September meeting have a very poor record in the (0-115) handicap at the October meeting, despite the fact that it is ideally timed just a fortnight later. It may be that they have 'trained off' at this point in the season.

6f: after the Wokingham handicap at the Royal Ascot meeting, there are no other 6f all-aged handicaps at Ascot. There is a 6f nursery at the September meeting, but no follow up opportunity at the final meeting in October.

7f: for all-aged horses there is one race at the first meeting (end of April); the other at the penultimate, Festival meeting (end of September). There is a 7f nursery at the final meeting. If the programme were changed, this distance would certainly be worth considering, as the straight, uphill finish seems tailor-made for specialists.

1m: the winner of the Royal Hunt Cup, the first 1m handicap here, rarely contests the Crocker Bulteel at the end of July. The winner of the Britannia Handicap (for three-year-olds) does not run again over a straight mile at Ascot during the season. The winner of the 3 y o fillies handicap at the Ascot Heath meeting (the Saturday of Royal Ascot week) is rarely seen in the all-aged fillies and mares handicap at the September meeting. Thus the evidence to date is insufficient. Remember that there are two 1m courses here: the Old Mile, which uses part of the round course; and the straight, Royal Hunt Cup mile.

1m 2f: there is a neatly placed series of 1m 2f handicaps at the July, September, and October meetings, but the results are poor, and this distance should be avoided.

1m 4f: the winners of the Bessborough Handicap (all-aged, 0-105) and the King George V Handicap (for three-year-olds, 0-105) do not usually run in the Ascot Handicap (all-aged, 0-110) at the September meeting, nor do previous winners. However, it would be worth continuing to check the results of this race, to see if a pattern emerges.

2m 45y: like the 1m 2f handicaps, there is a series ideally placed in July, September, and October. The difference here is that the results are fairly reasonable, although this is such an obvious pattern that the starting prices are poor, and there is little chance of a false-priced favourite.

## AYR

From our point of view, the programme of racing at Ayr can not be faulted. Meetings take place at suitable intervals in May, June, July, August, and September, and there are enough handicaps over the same distance. It is a good galloping course, and the going is usually consistent throughout the day - except at the Ayr Western meeting in September, when it can soften quite quickly. Although the course has no marked peculiarities, this does not automatically exclude the possibility that it could be suited to specialists - after all Ripon and Thirsk, both specialists' courses, are fairly similar in layout.

However, the record of course and distance winners is not good enough to regard it as a specialists' course. If you disagree, and decide to bet here, be very careful about the races at the Ayr Western meeting. These usually attract a higher standard of handicapper than at most Ayr races, and can beat the course specialist.

# How to Beat the Handicapper

## BATH

Winners at all distances here can win again. In particular, the 2m 1f 34y races offer good opportunities for specialists: the distance allied to the 3f uphill finish makes this a real test of stamina, which finds out horses which have only won over 2m. The course is not watered, and in a hot summer the going can get as hard as at any other course, so make sure that your selection has won on the going.

### 1995 selections

| Race 1202 | 22 May | 1m | VANBOROUGH LAD | W 8-1 |
| Race 1444 | 2 June | 2m 1f | INCHCAILLOCH | W 4-1 |

## BEVERLEY

Beverley is one of my 'star' courses. In most years, it has around 11 meetings, regularly spaced throughout the season; it has races at some odd distances, 7f 100y and 1m 100y, not found at other courses; and the going is usually predictable. Two handicaps are named after course specialists, RAPID LAD and TOUCH ABOVE, who both recorded more than 5 victories over the 1m 2f course. These two are not isolated examples - many other horses have shown form at this awkward course which they are not able to repeat elsewhere.

Here the course conformation does provide the clue. On the round course (all distances apart from 5f), the turns are quite sharp, but the field always seems to go a good gallop. A steep downhill bend leads into the 2½f uphill finish. Just for good measure, this is also set on a camber, to give the well-balanced horse with something in reserve a great opportunity to come from a long way off the pace.

The 5f course, which starts on an uphill spur of about 2½f, joins the main course with a distinct kink. Horses unused to the course sometimes cause problems here, which may explain why the 5f distance does not favour specialists.

The 1995 results were very disappointing, but they are not those of a typical year, since the average strike-rate here, 60%, is almost double that of 1995. As in many other cases, I can not emphasise enough that it is crucial to judge the results over a series of years, not just one season.

### 1995 selections

| Race 1036 | 12 May | 2m 35y | ROLLING THE BONES | W 11-10 |
| Race 1679 | 14 June | 7f 100y | EURO SCEPTIC | L 13-2 |
| Race 2222 | 7 July | 1m 100y | COUREUR | L 3-1 fav |

## BRIGHTON

If any course looks as if it ought to be a course and distance winner's paradise, it is Brighton. The first 3f are uphill; followed by a slight up and down; a marked downhill for 3f leading to a rise just before the final 100 yards, which catches out many short-runners.

There have been some well-known course specialists here, such as OPERATIC SOCIETY, but in the somewhat distant past. The programme offers plenty of opportunities to the course and distance winner, and 1m 4f winners in particular do have a promising record, judged on a small number of examples. The general problem at this course is a shortage of runners. Too many races attract small fields (five runners or fewer), especially during the months when the going is consistent. If the new management can attract larger fields, Brighton would be worth following closely.

## CARLISLE

This is a tough, galloping track. It has enough racing spaced at the right intervals to offer the course and distance specialist, but I have not been able to find enough selections here to judge whether it does really favour the specialist.

If you find otherwise, you must be particularly careful to check the going. Because the subsoil is clay, extremes of going (from heavy to hard) can be found in the same season. At Carlisle, 'hard going' means what it says, and since this is now rare on British racecourses, make sure that your selection can act on this going.

## CATTERICK

At all distances from 7f upwards, this is definitely a specialists' course, readily explained by the surface undulations and the sharp bends. Races are won in all sorts of styles here, and by horses in any position in the handicap: the deciding factor is previous course and distance success. Quick-actioned and manoeuvrable fillies and mares do well here.

This is not an easy course to ride: the northern jockeys who ride it regularly are at a definite advantage, while all but the very best apprentices find it too much of a test.

The 5f and 5f 212y races do not offer any advantages to course and distance winners, and the results show that they should be given a miss.

### 1995 selections

| Race 757 | 26 April | 1m 4f | KINOKO | L 10-1 |
| Race 2188 | 6 July | 7f | MAC'S TAXI | L 5-1 |

## CHEPSTOW

Chepstow has around ten meetings a season, invitingly spaced out - but not enough to tempt the course and distance specialist, it appears. In the straight, races are often run at a muddling sort of gallop, which may explain why few course and distance winners try again.

## CHESTER

On the face of it, Chester should be one of my 'star' courses. Just look at its conformation: a 1m 73y circle, flat throughout, with a straight 2f run-in. No other British racecourse is remotely like Chester.

In other respects, too, it seems to be ideal. There are enough meetings, since its programme has expanded in the last decade, so that there are now six meetings per season, well spaced out between May and September. The going is predictable, as it does not change much during the course of a meeting.

Yet my analysis of handicap results here shows that course and distance winners do not do well enough to justify identifying Chester as a specialists' course. After watching many races at Chester, I have come to the conclusion that even a horse well suited by the course is too likely to be 'boxed in' during the course of the race. No other course leads to so many 'hard luck' stories, and as nothing obliges you to bet here, I suggest you don't.

## DONCASTER

Along with Ripon and Thirsk, this is one of the more surprising specialists' courses. It is a spacious, left-handed course, with wide, sweeping turns, which would not seem to favour any particular kind of horse. The turf is excellent, and the course drains well, so that the going is extremely consistent. The programme of ten or so meetings spaced throughout the season offers regular opportunities for course and distance winners.

# How to Beat the Handicapper

Whatever the explanation, the facts speak for themselves. Jack Berry said of his sprint handicapper, AMRON, that he was a stone better here than at any other course. True enough - not only of AMRON but of other course-and-distance winners.

All handicaps are run over standard distances, with the exception of one race, the Portland Handicap, which is run over 5f 140y. This really is a specialist distance: in a fast-run race, it is just that bit too far for a 5f horse, and slightly too short for a winner at 6f. HELLO MISTER was the first horse for more than fifty years to win this race in successive years (1994 and 1995), but occasionally a winner can win two or three years later (DAWN'S DELIGHT, 1984 and 1987).

## 1995 selections

| | | | | |
|---|---|---|---|---|
| Race 1344 | 29 May | 1m | MIDNIGHT JAZZ | L 8-1 |
| Race 2117 | 2 July | 1m | BETTERGETON | W 5-1 |
| Race 3597 | 8 Sept | 5f | GENERAL SIR PETER | W 11-1 |
| Race 4197 | 21 Oct | 5f | NAME THE TUNE | L 13-2 |

## EPSOM

Beginning in 1991, Epsom has changed its programme. The Spring meeting has been dropped, and there are new meetings in July and August.

With its pronounced undulations, and the camber in the last furlong of the straight, Epsom looks as if it ought to be a specialists' course. At the Spring meeting (which is no longer held), there were one or two repeat winners of the same race, but the present programme tempts very few horses back after a first win.

Perhaps this is because many owners are unwilling to send their horses to Epsom, because of the uneven nature of the course. They will send them to the June meeting because they wish to have a runner on Derby or Oaks days, but not at the other, more socially humdrum meetings.

If a pattern does emerge here, you must remember to be cautious in two respects. The going can change quite quickly, and soft going can cause form upsets as it can be patchy in the home straight, with some jockeys electing to tack over to the stands' rail. Apprentices find it difficult to control their mounts' tendency to hang left with the prevailing right to left fall of the last furlong.

## FOLKESTONE

There certainly is enough racing here - fourteen meetings a year, from the third or fourth day of the season, to the very last day of the Flat.

This is an undemanding course, with easy turns, and minor undulations. The nearest I have come to finding a pattern here is in the 1m 1f 149y and 1m 4f handicaps which are run quite regularly throughout the season. Even so, I still have not found enough selections to be able to decide whether this course and distance genuinely favours specialists.

Be warned that the going here can change quickly during the course of a day. In wet weather, 'heavy' is a bit of a euphemism - 'quagmire' would be more accurate. Understandably, many jockeys hate riding here in such conditions, and results suffer accordingly.

## GOODWOOD

By contrast with today's crowded racing programme, it seems extraordinary that at one time Goodwood had only one meeting, of four days, at the end of July. It now has nine meetings, of eighteen days in all.

This is all to the good, as far as we are concerned. The course gives a definite advantage to specialists, although only at two distances - 6f and 1m 4f - have I found enough selections so far.

The 1m 4f course runs uphill, then undulates for several furlongs before turning sharply into the final 4f. It is probably the ability to negotiate this final bend at a reasonable speed which gives course specialists an edge.

Runners on the straight 6f sprint course, which meets the round course 4f out, face a steep hill at the start, which allows slow starters a respite. The 5f course falls for the first 200 yards and often catches out slow starters.

The July meeting is one of the most competitive meetings at any course. Course and distance form must be backed up by impressive wins at other leading courses if your selection is to have any chance at all. The course drains well, but unevenly. At the first (May) and last (September) meeting, the going can become soft quite quickly.

## 1995 selections

| Race 1241 | 24 May | 6f | CASTLEREA LAD | W 9-2 |
|---|---|---|---|---|
| Race 3615 | 8 Sept | 6f | NO EXTRAS | L 14-1 |

## HAMILTON

Both the straight 6f course and the loop course for longer distances favour specialists. In both cases, this can be accounted for by the severe gradients (up and down).

In any one season, however, looking for winners at Hamilton can be a frustrating affair. This is not because of lack of meetings (the usual programme has fourteen), but because of changes in the going and the frequent occurrence of small fields.

Because of its clay subsoil, the going is often heavy at the beginning and end of the season (March and September respectively). A winner on heavy going in March may return to the same distance and going six months later, having shown no form in an intervening period of good going. The conditions are right - but has it kept its form?

Equally frustrating, a good winner runs over the right distance and going, within a few weeks of its previous victory, only to find itself in a small field. Will the race be run at a fast enough pace to ensure a result for the form book?

Who knows? The answer is anybody's guess, and there are more clear cut opportunities to be found in other races.

## 1995 selections

| Race 3852 | 25 Sept | 1m 4f 17y | CHANTRY BEATH | L 3-1 |
|---|---|---|---|---|

## HAYDOCK

The sprint handicaps run on the straight 6f course have attracted a number of successful course specialists. They are a reliable test, as there is a constant rise in the final 4f.

The races from 7f 40y up to 1m 3f 200y do not favour course specialists, perhaps because the field is still bunched when it reached the sharp bend into the straight. In 1m 3f 200y races, there is more time for the field to spread out. Even so, it is still not possible to say whether or not this is a specialists course and distance. There is not enough data on the longer distance handicaps to make a judgement.

Haydock is on the wetter side of the country, and at the beginning and the end of the season, the going gets very heavy. For this reason, in the longer distance races (7f 40y upwards), jockeys negotiate the final bend very cautiously. The slow pace of such races means that their form is worthless.

# How to Beat the Handicapper

1995 selections

Race 1304         27 May    5f       LORD HIGH ADMIRAL         W 10-1

## KEMPTON

Kempton begins with a bang with its early season meetings, but goes out with a whimper later on in the season. The spacing of the handicaps throughout the season, and the allocation of handicaps of various levels and distances, means that there are very few opportunities for course and distance winners. Although the rather tight 'round' course and the more galloping Jubilee course differ in character, neither is worth considering as a specialists' course.

## LEICESTER

Over the years, Leicester has been a very good course for finding course and distance winners, at distances of 1m 8y upwards.

For races over 1m 3f 183y, the longest distance here, and 1m 1f 218y, they run right-handed round easy bends, to join a 4½f run-in. The last four furlongs is a stiff uphill test, which ensures reliable form. The 1m races begin on a straight extension to the main course.

There are fourteen meetings during the season, with the final four (from the first week in September) being neatly grouped to give a good chance to course specialists. In recent years, MISTY SILKS has been an outstanding performer here, winning 4 races over 1m.

Watch out for soft going here, especially at the beginning and the end of the season. It really does make life difficult for horses which do not act on this type of going, while giving a great advantage to horses which have had very limited opportunities earlier in the summer. Unfortunately, in 1995 there were no selections here, almost certainly because of the unusually firm going at the end of the season.

1995 selections

None.

## LINGFIELD

Since Lingfield laid out an All-Weather Track, racing on the turf course seems to have gone into a decline. It used to offer possibilities for course and distance specialists, but it no longer does so. This is a pity, because since the improvements in drainage were carried out, the going is much more consistent and does not undergo such abrupt changes.

## MUSSELBURGH (formerly Edinburgh)

Like Brighton, but for different reasons, Musselburgh is often plagued by small fields. It may be that trainers consider it rather inaccessible, but it does have up to twelve meetings a season, which offer plenty of opportunities for repeat course and distance wins. I have not found enough selections here to be able to judge whether or not this is a specialists' course.

## NEWBURY

Newbury is one of those courses which looks as if it does not give the course and distance winner an edge - and it doesn't. The course is a 15f left-handed oval, with easy bends leading to a 5f home straight. There are slight undulations in the straight, but otherwise this is a flat, featureless course.

Most winners seem to be 'passing through', and I do not remember any course specialist recording a significant number of wins. There are not enough selections here to assess whether a course and distance win is a significant pointer.

I suspect that if more of the 7f handicaps were run on the straight course, rather than the round course, they might be a better bet. In the current programme, five are run on the round course, and only two (including one apprentice handicap) on the straight, which seems to be reserved for stakes races.

## NEWCASTLE

A new management team here will, I hope, be able to revitalise the course. This would be very well deserved, since, for the form student, Newcastle is one of the best. The 1m 6f left-handed oval has a 4f run-in with a gradual rise to the winning post. It is a fair and very testing track. Races up to 7f are set on a straight extension to the main course.

There is no other track like this on the 'northern circuit': Beverley and Pontefract have an uphill finish, but do not allow for such a strong gallop in the earlier stages; Carlisle is almost as testing, but does not attract the same class of horse. Doncaster, Ripon, Thirsk, and York are all flat courses. Newcastle is the northern equivalent of Newmarket, in encouraging a good gallop at the beginning of races, and testing the faint-hearted with a strenuous uphill finish.

Races at all distances are suitable for the course and distance specialist. There are only 9 meetings here, but the programme is well organised. There are three good class handicaps at the end of June: the Gosforth Park Cup (5f); the Sprint Trophy (6f); and the Northumberland Plate (2m 19y). These races usually attract very competitive fields, and it is not enough to be a course and distance specialist, since a selection must have good recent form at a leading course such as Haydock, Newmarket or Sandown.

The going can be testing at any point in the season. In the back straight, the sprinklers leave the outside third of the track unwatered, so that if it rains shortly after watering, the outside ground is much faster.

### 1995 selections

| Race 2060 | 30 June | 5f | PRINCESS OBERON | L 6-1 |
| Race 3368 | 26 Aug | 1m | SCARABEN | W 15-2 |

## NEWMARKET

I have run out of superlatives to describe Newmarket, so completely does it deserve its title of 'Headquarters'.

Both courses (July and Rowley Mile) have the same general characteristics: wide, galloping tracks, with testing uphill finishes. Course and distance winners have a great advantage over winners which have not won here. Horses which run well on turning tracks invariably find the open, staring spaces of Newmarket too daunting. Easy winners on flat or downhill tracks quickly run out of steam when faced with the final climb.

There are plenty of opportunities throughout the season: so much so that in most seasons Newmarket gives this system more selections than any other course. Over a longer period, the system has the highest winning strike-rate of any course.

Do remember, though, that the courses are different, and, for form purposes, not interchangeable. The July course has the steepest finish of any Flat course, rising 18 feet at 1/46. The finish of the Rowley Mile is gentler only by comparison, rising 11 feet at 1/65. It is always worth making sure when checking the field for a July course handicap, that 'CD' (course and distance winner) does not mistakenly refer to a win on

# How to Beat the Handicapper

the Rowley Mile course.

The two major handicaps at Newmarket, the Cambridgeshire (1m 1f: first October meeting) and the Cesarewitch (2m 2f: second October meeting) should be avoided, if you are looking for a course and distance selection. The only exception (for the very patient) is a previous winner (not necessarily in the previous year) of the Cambridgeshire. Generally, these races are so competitive, that previous winners are too high in the handicap.

## 1995 selections

| | | | | |
|---|---|---|---|---|
| Race 661 | 18 April | 1m 6f | TUDOR ISLAND | W 7-1 |
| Race 934 | 7 May | 6f | MASTER PLANNER | W 9-1 |
| Race 2746 | 28 July | 6f | MISS ARAGON | W 9-1 |
| Race 2948 | 5 Aug | 7f | CADEAUX TRYST | L 7-1 |

## NOTTINGHAM

A track without marked characteristics, being flat throughout, with easy turns. Its 'neutral' character is borne out in the results for course and distance selections, which are too few to make it worthwhile taking a closer interest in this course.

## PONTEFRACT

This is one of the odder-looking tracks. Although it is the second longest Flat course in Britain (about 2 miles round), the run-in is one of the shortest, at just over 2f. With some tricky turns, two rises and two falls until the final steep rise to the finish, this looks as if it was consciously designed to be a specialists' track, and this is borne out by results.

As at Beverley, the awkward turn into the straight may explain why the sprint distances do not favour course and distance winners, and lead to some shock results. Concentrate on the races from 1m 4y, and further.

In a dry summer, the going can get hard here. Very few horses can really act on this going, so ensure that your selection is one of them.

## 1995 selections

| | | | | |
|---|---|---|---|---|
| Race 841 | 1 May | 1m 2f 6y | OBELOS | L 9-4 |

## REDCAR

Redcar offers no favours to any particular type of horse, nor to course and distance winners. It is a long, flat, narrow, left-handed oval, with sharp bends leading to a 5f run-in.

Your analysis of the results may lead you to a different conclusion, but I have not found enough selections here to make a decision. If you do think that course and distance winners can be followed here, be careful when analysing the Zetland Gold Cup (1m 2f, end of May), which has been won by some useful handicappers in recent years (ERADICATE 1990; WAINWRIGHT 1994).

Starting from 1990, more 7f races have been introduced into the programme, so that there is now a conveniently placed series, mid-July, end of August, end of September, and the beginning of October. To date, the results are encouraging. In races with a clear selection, there have been three winners out of four (the latest being QUILLING, Race 4236 24 October 1995); and in one race with two selections, they finished first and second.

# How to Beat the Handicapper

## RIPON

There is no apparent reason why Ripon should suit course and distance winners, but it most certainly does. With the exception of a slight dip about a furlong out, the course is a flat, right-handed oval, with quite sharp bends. The 6f course is set on a straight extension.

The final meeting here is at the end of August, but up to that point there are eleven meetings, with enough chances for the course and distance winner to gain a repeat victory. The turf is good, and well-drained, so that the going is rarely worse than soft.

The only handicap here for which a course and distance win is not by itself enough is the Great St. Wilfrid (6f, towards the end of August). Good form from higher class courses, such as Newmarket or York, is essential.

### 1995 selections

| | | | | |
|---|---|---|---|---|
| Race 535 | 5 April | 6f | PALACEGATE TOUCH | W 9-1 |
| Race 1414 | 31 May | 6f | THE SCYTHIAN | W 10-1 |

## SALISBURY

Salisbury is a mystery course. It has a testing uphill finish of almost four furlongs, and the form shown here is a reliable guide to performance elsewhere, particularly on similar courses. Why it is not as reliable at Salisbury itself is hard to understand, but the fact of the matter is that, to date, course and distance selections have too low a strike-rate to make this a specialists' track.

## SANDOWN

A 'star' course for generating course and distance winners, season after season. In reality, it is two courses.

The separate 5f course set inside the main course rises steadily uphill throughout. There is no other 5f course like it, and it suits specialists admirably. Almost every season, you will read about a hopeful, who has not won over the course and distance: 'Has done well over 6f at X, and Sandown's stiff five should suit him.' It doesn't, as the relentless uphill grind is a completely different proposition from running over an easy 6f. There have been several specialists over this course and distance, the most recent being MAGIC ORB (1993, 1994).

The 1m 5f round course also has a testing finish of almost 4f uphill. This is very much a specialists course at all distances bar one - there are too few races over the unusual distance of 1m 3f 9y to determine whether the course and distance winner has an advantage or not.

There is only one handicap in the current programme, the Royal Hong Kong Jockey Club Trophy (1m 2f 7y, first July meeting) which requires course and distance form to be supplemented by a good win at another high-class course.

### 1995 selections

| | | | | |
|---|---|---|---|---|
| Race 1753 | 16 June | 1m 2f 7y | SPECIAL DAWN | W 9-4 |
| Race 1794 | 17 June | 1m 6f | EMBRACING | W 15-8 |

## THIRSK

Thirsk is one of those northern tracks (the other two Doncaster and Ripon) with no visible topographical oddities, which regularly turn up course and distance winners.

It is a 1m 2f left-handed oval, with easy bends leading to a 4f run-in. Apart from the slight undulations in the home straight, it is completely flat throughout.

# How to Beat the Handicapper

Although the last meeting is rather early in the season (at the beginning of September), there is a regular well-spaced programme of nine meetings in the preceding five months. The course is within easy reach of all the leading northern stables, which may explain why winners here frequently try for, and usually succeed in, a repeat performance.

The turf here is of good quality, and well maintained, so that extremes of going are rarely encountered.

## 1995 selections

| Race 1179 | 20 May | 7f | HI NOD | L 6-1 |
| Race 1844 | 20 June | 1m 4f | LOOKINGFORARAINBOW | L 5-2 |
| Race 3357 | 25 Aug | 5f | KALAR | W 5-1 |

## WARWICK

The 1m 6f left-handed course is nearly circular, with difficult bends leading to a run-in of over 3f. However, the home straight is wide enough to allow plenty of room for a challenge from quite a long way off the pace.

Over the shorter distances (5f - 7f), the final bend has too much of an effect on the result, but races of 1m upwards are very suited to course and distance winners. MYFONTAINE recorded his seventh course and distance win over 1m 2f 169y on 12 June (Race 1658).

## 1995 selections

| Race 1543 | 7 June | 1m 2f 169y | MYFONTAINE | W 9-4 |

## WINDSOR

Windsor is the only Flat course formed in a figure of eight. The 5f run-in is almost straight, so that horses which have kept their balance and run economically round the bends, have plenty of time for a challenge.

At distances from 1m 67y to the longest distance of 1m 3f 135y, the unique course configuration definitely favours course specialists, from QUORTINA in the early seventies right down to the present day.

In the summer, the going is usually reasonably good here, rarely being hard or heavy. From the end of April to the end of August, there is one meeting per week, usually on Monday evenings. There has been a down-turn in selections in the last two years - whether or not this is a reflection of a temporary decline in Windsor's popularity, caused by the rather inconvenient layout for spectators, is hard to say.

## 1995 selections

| Race 1513 | 5 June | 1m 3f 135y | SCENIC DANCER | L 7-2 |

## YARMOUTH

Like Brighton, Yarmouth is another course which has suffered a decline in popularity caused by factors which have nothing to do with racing fashion, i.e. its demise as a holiday centre. Trainers seem more inclined to use the course as a testing ground for other courses, than to look for repeat handicap wins. Consequently, I have not found enough course and distance winners here to decide whether or not this is a specialists' course.

This is one of the few courses with a straight, flat 7f distance. Unfortunately, the races are rather unevenly distributed throughout the season, making for few opportunities.

## YORK

The course layout, a wide, flat, left-handed oval, is unremarkable, but I am not convinced that this is the reason why course and distance winners do not have an outstandingly good record here.

The reason certainly is not the pattern of the handicaps. Although there are only six meetings here, from May to October, the handicaps are suitably spaced to offer opportunities to the course and distance winner.

There could be two reasons for the York not being a clear-cut case of a specialists' track, and it is difficult to say whether one is more important than the other. Firstly, York is the leading northern course, and owners try hard to have winners here, making most handicaps (particularly the sprints) rather competitive.

The other reason is that the going at York is very unpredictable. It can change within a matter of hours, and when it does it inevitably produces shock results, especially as the course does not drain evenly. Even on going which is both consistent and good to firm, form upsets are fairly frequent.

If you disagree, and wish to back course and distance winners here, remember that the August meeting is very much a cut above the rest, so that you can not rely only on course and distance form. In particular, avoid the 1m 6f Ebor handicap, which so often goes to a 'dark horse'. The 1995 winner, SANMARTINO, had only won one previous race, a 1m 2f maiden stakes at Haydock, on 27 May. His clever trainer, Barry Hills, trained him to perfection, but a form student could not predict this kind of result.

My analysis of results from York shows that you should consider a course and distance winner only under the following three conditions:

1. avoid the August meeting.

2. the going is good to firm, and the weather is settled.

3. the candidate won the same race in the previous season.

Even under these conditions, course and distance winners have a lower strike-rate at York than at any other course. If you are prepared to accept the risk, the betting market is strong here, and there are also frequent false-priced favourites, with a very high losing strike-rate.

### 1995 selections

Race 1106      17 May    5f        SADDLEHOME      L 7-1

## IRISH COURSES

## THE CURRAGH

Ireland's biggest, toughest course: 2m round, with the most testing uphill finish of any British or Irish course. Of all the distances here, the 7f and 1m races provide the most selections. In 1995, I found the defeat of BAYDUR the most puzzling of all the season's results, especially given that he was trained by Dermot Weld. The victory of THE BOWER at 8-1 in the Irish Cambridgeshire (9 September; not analysed here), was the most frustrating, given that I thought that an equally good case could be made out for MEGLIO CHE POSSO, so that there was no selection.

# How to Beat the Handicapper

19 Aug    7f       BAYDUR           L 3-1

## GALWAY

This is a tight, undulating course, only 1m round, but it is the sharp rise to the finish which gives the specialists an advantage. Other courses in Ireland have a similar layout, but the programme of racing here is much better suited to the specialist, with a 6-day July Festival, and two meetings in September.

The Festival meeting is so popular with owners and trainers that horses often run again within one or two days. If you do not watch the races yourself, then you will not be able to judge whether a course and distance winner should be a selection, because the *Irish Field* will not have appeared in time. A case in point was KAKASHDA, who won two 1m 4f handicaps at the 1995 Festival.

However, in future, it is possible that SIS will transmit Irish racing. Should this happen, even if you do not watch any other races from Ireland, try not to miss the Galway Festival races.

### 1995 selections

13 Sept   1m 100y  GLASDERRYMORE L 12-1

## LEOPARDSTOWN

The regular programme of racing here really gets going from the middle of June and runs on at well-spaced intervals until the end of October.

A left-handed oval track of fourteen furlongs, this is a generous-sized track by Irish standards, and, combined with a 2½f uphill finish, it sets a distinctive test which favours the course and distance specialist at all distances. As with The Curragh, the going here tends to be much firmer than on other Irish courses. Horses which have run well on the softer ground prevalent in the west regularly find this firmer going not at all to their liking.

### 1995 selections

13 Aug    7f       LOVING CONTRACT           L 7-1
28 Oct    1m 2f    SOFT SPOT         W no SP returned

## TRALEE

Although this is rather similar in layout to other Irish courses, being a tight, left-handed 1m 1f circuit, it not only has a testing uphill finish, but, perhaps more importantly, it has a programme structure which gives the course and distance winner a chance. The 5-day Festival (end of August) is preceded by a meeting earlier in the season; and previous seasons' winners can take advantage of suitable preparatory races at other difficult courses.

### 1995 selections

27 Aug    1m 4f    MAGIC FEELING    W 9-2

## LIST OF SPECIALIST COURSES/DISTANCES

Bath:                   all distances
Beverley:               all distances from 7f 100y upwards
Catterick:              all distances from 7f upwards
Doncaster:              all distances

# How to Beat the Handicapper

| | |
|---|---|
| Goodwood: | 6f; 1m 4f |
| Hamilton: | all distances |
| Haydock: | 5f; 6f; 1m 4f |
| Leicester: | all distances from 1m upwards |
| Newcastle: | all distances |
| Newmarket (July): | all distances |
| Newmarket (Rowley): | all distances |
| Pontefract: | all distances from 1m 4y upwards |
| Ripon: | all distances |
| Sandown: | all distances bar 1m 3f 9y |
| Thirsk: | all distances |
| Warwick: | all distances from 1m upwards |
| Windsor: | all distances from 1m 67y upwards |
| York: | all distances (g-f only; same race winners only) |
| Galway: | all distances |
| Leopardstown: | all distances |
| The Curragh: | all distances |
| Tralee: | all distances |

# CHAPTER THREE

# THE TEN MINUTE SYSTEM

Having noted that there are handicaps over a suitable course and distance, what do you do next? The first step is the quickest: if these handicaps have attracted five runners or fewer, they should be ignored, as such races too often lead to misleading results.

After finding a suitable race at a suitable course, what is the next stage? The selection process can be sub-divided as follows:

identifying a course and distance qualifier;
checking the qualifier's form credentials;
weighing up the opposition.

This chapter will now describe how to follow this process through to a conclusion. It may seem rather complicated at first, but with just a little practice, it does not take long. Over a series of 500 races, I found that the average time required is ten minutes. This is an average: in 1995 I found that the lengthiest analysis took forty minutes (see chapter 5, Race 4267 28 October), while the briefest was five minutes (see chapter 5, Race 1036 12 May).

On some days, there are no races to analyse at all; on average, there about 40 races per season, that is, just over one per week. This does not mean that they occur with clockwork regularity. You will find that there are two or even more weeks when there are no races to analyse. In 1995, the longest gap between races was four calendar weeks. It is a sign that this is a system which has identified a pattern, that these fall at unequal intervals.

How can a basic qualifier be identified? First, I check that the candidate has won a handicap over the course and distance. I discount winning a non-handicap, as, although this may seem to indicate a liking for the course, such races are generally not very testing.

A course and distance winner which has since won at a longer distance, so that he is now being put back in distance, should be discounted.

Secondly, I verify that a horse has won a 'proper' handicap, i.e. not an amateur, apprentice, claiming, or selling handicap, over the course and distance. 'Nurseries', i.e. handicaps for two-year-olds, I regard as 'proper' handicaps.

Thirdly, has he only won races in small fields? 'Small' in this context means five runners or fewer. If he has won races in the past against six or more, but this season has only won races in a field of five or fewer, I eliminate this candidate from the reckoning, on the grounds that these are unreliable races. The only exception to this rule is the same race winner.

Fourthly, I check the race reports in both *Raceform Update* and *Sporting Life*, and if any of the following words or phrases appear, I eliminate the horse concerned:

all out
driven (at any point in the race)
driven out
flat out (at any point in the race)
gamely (at any point in the race)
hard ridden (at any point in the race)
just held on

pressure (at any point in the race)
ran on gamely
ran on under pressure
stayed on under pressure

Remember that you are not looking for horses which win with a great deal in hand, so as to be able to deceive the Handicapper. It is the ability to win over the course and distance, not the style of the win, which is crucial with such horses. Instead of looking *positively* for a certain kind of style (as in my previous two books: *How to Win at Handicap Racing* Raceform 1990; *Bigger Profits from Handicap Races* Raceform 1994), I look *negatively* for indications that this is the limit of a horse's ability.

This may seem too restrictive, but in fact it only excludes about 35% of all winners. I have found that it is essential to use two sources, as a double check; but I have not found any two sources to be any better than any other two - just use whichever you find easiest. The two which I use are *Sporting Life* and *Raceform Update*. Remember that if you use the *Sporting Life*, the reports in the *Sporting Life Weekender* are by the same race readers, so that these are not two different sources.

If you can not check two sources, don't bet. It happens once or twice a season that the second report in the *Raceform Update* is not available, because the race has been run very close to the date of publication. Of course, for the purposes of keeping your records up to date, you can analyse such a race and note the result.

There are three exceptions to the two-sources rule. If you have watched the race yourself, you must always have faith in you own judgement. The other exception is that you must always read very carefully *Reflections in Running* (in the *Raceform Update*) and *A Week at the Races* (*Sporting Life Weekender*). If they praise a winner highly, by noting that he won 'decisively', 'impressively', 'any amount in hand', then ignore reports from other sources which suggest that he had to be 'hard ridden' or 'driven out'. This happens only once or twice a season (e.g. OBELOS, Race 676 19 April Pontefract 1m 2f 9y).

For racing in Ireland, it is not always possible to find two accounts of a race. The *Racing Post* and the *Sporting Life* do not always report on every handicap, and even for the more important handicaps, their reporting tends towards the minimal. However, *The Irish Field* (PO Box 74, 11-15 D'Olier Street, Dublin 2) gives such a thorough account of every handicap race that there is no need to look for another source.

At this point, if the process seems rather cumbersome, may I bring an element of relief by referring to the factors which do not have to be checked at any point.

You do not need to watch any races whatsoever. This means that if you do not have much time to watch races, or feel that you do not have very good race-reading skills, you can work entirely from newspaper reports. Of course, if you are confident of your ability to read a race, you must let your own judgements over-ride those of reporters. Remember that you are not looking for horses with a late finish, but you are seeking to exclude those which have been hard ridden or driven at any point during the race, or which look at the end of their tether in the final stages.

You do not need to know anything about the ability of the trainer, as these horses train themselves. The level of competence required on the part of a trainer to nurture an improving horse, so as to produce him at the right moment to run up a sequence in handicaps, is of quite a different order.

It is true that some trainers do have a good record with course and distance winners, by running them at the 'wrong' courses and distances until their handicap mark has fallen to a winnable level. However, it is not necessary to know who these trainers are - what matters is the horse's liking for a particular course and distance. With trainers, it is especially important not to try 'second-guessing' their intentions - is the trainer getting him 'ready' for today? - when what matters is the right combination of circumstances for the horse.

You do not need to look at the name of the jockey, as these horses run themselves and do not require particularly inspired handling. However, I would avoid backing a horse ridden by a 5lb or 7lb apprentices, as generally these riders do not ride consistently enough.

With one reservation, you do not have to worry about the qualifier's age, as course and distance winners can and do win at any age. The one reservation is the handicap mark. If a horse aged eight years and upwards is running off a higher mark than that from which he has won at any time in the past, he should be excluded. Horses of this age can return to something like their best form, but they are very unlikely to improve.

Time is not a factor, as, except for the highest-class handicaps (which you are very unlikely to be analysing in any case), it is outweighed by the course and distance advantage.

Finally, you do not need to check the story line, i.e. is there any event in the horse's past, such as being gelded, lightly-raced, or changing trainer, which explains why he has run so well recently? The very fact of having won a course and distance handicap is a story sufficient in itself.

It is not at all essential to keep lists of course and distance winners, as you can wait until the day of the race to see if there are any qualifiers. Look through your daily racing paper, to see if there are any course and distance winners at specified courses; and then look back to another source, to see if they should be eliminated or can be retained. This may mean looking back through the form book for previous seasons, or whatever records you keep of previous seasons' racing. So if in 1995, you see that a horse won over the course and distance in 1993, go back to the 1993 form, and see if it is still a qualifier.

If you find a course and distance winner which has not been eliminated by any of the tests set out above it can be retained, check the following points, beginning with the most frequent types of elimination, and ending with the least frequent.

Recent form: the main season. If, from the Epsom Derby meeting onwards, a course and distance winner has not won a handicap (and not just a race) this season, then eliminate it immediately. If it has won a handicap in an acceptable style, even if not over the course and distance, then carry on checking.

Recent form: early season. In the first ten weeks of the season (which is usually up to the end of May), very little form is available. If the horse has not won this season, you need to check back since there are two cases in which you can select a a course and distance winner which has not won this season.

First, a horse which won over the course and distance at the end (October/November) of the previous season (for an example, see chapter 5, Race 661 18 April Newmarket TUDOR ISLAND).

Secondly, a horse which has won the same race in the previous season. Some horses run well at the beginning of the season, and then run frequently but badly for the rest of the season, so that their handicap mark falls to what it was at the beginning of the season. PALACEGATE TOUCH (Race 535 5 April Ripon) was a classic example.

In this case, you can back a horse first and second time out, providing that in the previous season it won first time out, or is the type of horse which runs well when fresh. Here you must look very closely at the handicap mark.

This is by far the riskiest type of selection following this system, and there is not really any way of minimising the risk. Some trainers (e.g. Jack Berry) specialise in placing horses in this way, and you should keep for reference the copies of *Raceform Update* or *Sporting Life Weekender* which carry interviews with him. If you are a good judge of a horse's condition, you may be able to see for yourself that the horse is fit and well. In itself, this is not a conclusive test - even if he looks fit, he may not be quite up to the standard of the previous season.

In this period, the easiest case is when a horse is noted (again, you must use two sources) as running well, without winning. If he runs in the same race, off a mark near that of his previous victory, then this is a possible selection, subject to further tests (e.g. GOOD HAND (Race 1268 25 May Newcastle)).

If a possible selection does not fall into one of these categories, rule it out immediately.

## SUITABILITY TO THE GOING

Has the possible selection won on today's going or similar going? The horse's record on different types of going can be seen at a glance in *Raceform Form-Book* (for previous seasons) or in *Sporting Life* (its entire career). Here your aim is not to guess whether a horse may be suited by a type of going on which it is unproven, but to look realistically at its previous record.

To do so, I classify types of going as follows:

1. heavy
2. soft/yielding/good to soft
3. good
4. good to firm
5. firm/hard

The easiest case is where a horse has won a number of races, but never on the type of going for today's race. In this case, it should be eliminated without hesitation.

The next easiest is that of a horse which may have won, say, six races, of which five are on good or good to firm going, and one on soft going. This suggests that it has a preference for good or good to firm, and on any other type of going it should be eliminated.

The most difficult case to weigh up involves types 3 and 4. To a certain extent these are interchangeable. With a lightly-raced horse which has only won on good going, it is not always clear that it will be suited by good to firm: if you are risk-averse, then it is best to leave alone.

## RECENT FORM

When a course and distance winner shows acceptable form (i.e. winning a handicap over the distance, even if not necessarily over the course), and when it runs again over the course and distance, you can write off any other form it shows within this period at other courses/distances/going/types of races.

Do not worry if this means considering the chances of a horse with form figures such as 100000. For example, the 1 could represent a win on soft going in a 1m 2f handicap at Beverley, and the discouraging series of zeros record unplaced runs in a 1m 2f handicap at York on firm going, a 1m 2f handicap at Catterick on good going, a 1m 4f handicap at Ripon on soft going, a 1m 2f handicap at Thirsk on good going, and a 1m 2f claimer at Newcastle on soft going. If within ninety days, this horse returns to a 1m 2f handicap at Beverley on soft going, it has a live chance.

You may have the additional bonus that in the meantime its handicap mark has fallen from the level it reached after the Beverley win. Say that it wins at Beverley by a comfortable two lengths, off a mark of 65. The Handicapper is quite impressed, and raises the mark to 70, accounting this to be equivalent to a five-length win. After his four losing runs, the Handicapper relents, and reduces the mark to 67.

If, next time out, the horse runs at Beverley over 1m 2f on soft going, not only does he have course, distance and going in his favour, but also he is on a more reasonable handicap mark, thanks to his poor performances under unsuitable conditions.

# How to Beat the Handicapper

Recent form: the ninety day rule. If a horse has shown no worthwhile form in the last ninety (calendar, not racing) days, it should be eliminated. This does not necessarily mean winning form, but it should mean running well when finishing close up. For example, a horse might win a handicap at the beginning of May, and then be given a mid-season break to come back at the end of September. You should wait to see if it shows some worthwhile (i.e. winning) form before giving it more serious consideration.

Recent form: handicap mark. If within the last ninety days, a possible selection runs over the course, distance and going, and is defeated, eliminate it immediately even if it is now running off a lower handicap mark.

## PUNISHED BY THE HANDICAPPER?

If a horse wins in an acceptable style, he may sometimes appear to be severely punished by the Handicapper. For example, a horse may win by a length, for which the handicap allowance at that distance is 1lb, but the Handicapper increases the winner's mark by 7lb. You should apply the handicap scale literally, following the standard weight for distance scale:

| | |
|---|---|
| 5f, 6f | 3lb for one length |
| 7f, 8f | 2lb for one length |
| 1m 1f + | 1lb for one length |

Fractions of a length are calculated in proportion.

If you find that your possible selection is more than 7lb 'over-rated' by the Handicapper, it is best to leave well alone. The advantage of a course and distance win can only outweigh an increase in handicap mark to a certain extent.

## TOO HIGH IN THE HANDICAP

This applies particularly to older horses. A horse aged eight years and older may win if on a mark at or below a previous winning mark, but will find it very difficult to win if he is rated above his best previous winning mark.

Five, six and seven-year-olds present a more difficult problem - one of the few cases where judgement is required. If they are well-exposed handicappers which have run frequently for two or three seasons, it will be easy to identify their limiting mark, above which they are unable to win. Only if there is a story line (such as being gelded or changing trainer) which suggests that they may be able to win above their previous limit, should you consider such horses as a selection.

There were only two cases in 1995, one of each type.

There were no special circumstances to suggest that MASTER PLANNER could win when rated above his previous limit (Race 1100 York 16 May). Now a six-year-old, in 1993 he had run in 15 races, and in the following year 14 races. His form was well exposed, and there was no reason to suppose he could surpass previous performances.

SCARABEN (Race 3368 Newcastle 26 August) was a different matter. As a four-year-old in 1992, trained by Hugh Collingridge, he had only run three times; in 1993, he did not appear on the racecourse at all. Trained by Steve Kettlewell from 1994, he had begun to show improvement. Apparently, he was recovering from an earlier injury, and continued to improve in 1995, even as a seven-year-old.

I also investigated that other possibility, that a horse might be too *low* in the handicap. Before carrying out the analysis, I thought it likely that horses in the lowest quarter of the handicap range (35-55) might be more consistent than horses in the top quarter (95-115). This was not the case, and they were as consistent as horses from any range within the handicap system. I also thought that more selections would come from the lower end of the handicap, but in fact they were fairly evenly distributed across the complete handicap spectrum.

## TOO HIGH IN THE WEIGHTS
However strongly built, any horse which has to carry more than 10st has an impossible burden. At the moment there are very few examples, but with the raising of the minimum weight to 7st 10lb in 1996, this may become more frequent. There was only one example in 1995 (Race 1658 12 June Warwick MYFONTAINE).

Those types listed so far are the most frequent. Finally, there are a number of infrequent types, which fortunately are very easy to identify.

## APPRENTICE RIDERS
Even Lester Piggott and Frankie Dettori were 7lb and 5lb claimers once, but I still think it is a good idea to give horses ridden by claimers in these categories a miss. But if you are really impressed by a claimer, and he has won on the horse concerned, you may decide differently.

In my view, the 3lb claimers are generally much more reliable, but it is still essential that they have previously won on the horse they are riding today. There are usually only one or two cases a year to consider.

## WINNER OF A SMALL FIELD RACE
Races with five or fewer runners are very unreliable. If a horse has only won over the course and distance in this type of race, it should not be considered; and if its only win (s) in the current season have been in small fields, it should also be discounted.

## HAS ONLY WON A FILLIES/FILLIES AND MARES HANDICAP
Once they run into form, fillies and mares can strike a purple patch - but if they have never won against colts, they are an unknown quantity, and should be avoided. There were no examples in 1995.

At the end of this process, you will have identified the course, distance and going winners which have sound, recent form, and which are in a reasonable position in the handicap. If there are two such winners, you should not attempt to weigh up the differences between them, but should leave the race alone. In most seasons, this will happen only once or twice. A three qualifiers race is exceptional, and should of course be avoided.

So far I have been using the process of elimination to identify a course and distance selection. Now I use the same process to weigh up the opposition.

## WEIGHING UP THE OPPOSITION
My aim is to divide the opposition into three categories: runners which can be discounted; those which can not be discounted; and 'dark horses'.

The method is simple in principle, but sometimes laborious in practice. It consists of: simple elimination; and complex elimination.

Simple elimination consists of excluding those horses which fall in the following categories:

horses which have never won a race;

horses which have not won a handicap;

horses which have not won a handicap over the distance of the race;

horses which have only won amateurs, apprentices, or selling handicaps.

A remarkable number of the runners will fall into the first two categories, i.e. horses which have never won a race or never won a handicap. In the 46 British and Irish races analysed in this book, there were a total of 641 runners. Horses which had not won a race or had not won a handicap made up 37.5% of the runners, but won only 10.8% of the races. By contrast, course and distance winners made up 14% of the runners, but won 54.3% of the races.

These are not exceptional results, as 1995 was an average year. The proportion of losing non-handicap/non race-winners remains fairly constant, as does the proportion of course and distance winners.

There are two more simple cases: the runners which have won only amateurs, apprentices, or selling races over the distance; and the runners which have won a handicap, but not over the distance of the race. In the latter category, of the races analysed in this book, 19.7% of the runners won 13% of the races - not quite so striking a discrepancy as compared to the runners which have not won a race or handicap, but still a significant bias.

So far the process is straightforward, takes hardly any time, and is rather tedious. A more complex elimination is required to evaluate the chances of the other runners, the distance winners. You must check the following categories, in any order you like (given here alphabetically, simply for the reader's convenience). Most of these checks are exactly the same as those applied to course and distance winners, but they are set out again below to familiarise the reader with the procedure.

## GOING
Has the horse won on today's going or similar going?

I group types of going as follows:

1. heavy
2. soft/yielding/good to soft
3. good
4. good to firm
5. firm/hard

Types 1, 2, and 5. If a horse has only won on one of these types, and today's going is not of this type; or if today's going is one of these types, and the horse has only won on types 3 and 4, then I strike him out immediately, and write against his name: 'unsuited by the going'.

Types 3 and 4. To a certain extent, these types of going are interchangeable. If a horse is has won on one of these types, but is an unknown quantity on the other type; and if he can not be eliminated on other grounds, I write: 'unknown quantity on the going, but can not be discounted.'

Type 5 used to be much more frequent before courses were watered regularly. Nowadays it only occurs at some courses - Bath, Carlisle, and Pontefract. It really is different from firm going, with which it is sometimes confused.

**Has only won a fillies/fillies and mares handicap.** Fillies which have not shown they can win against colts and geldings are to be discounted - it is not clear that they relish the rough and tumble of racing against the more aggressive, strongly built animals.

# How to Beat the Handicapper

**Has only won races in small fields**: 'small' in this context means five runners or fewer. If it has won races in the past against six or more, but this season, has only won races against five, I am still inclined to discount its chances on the grounds that these are unreliable races.

**Has not won a handicap this season**. This applies from the beginning of June. Runners in races after this date which have not won this season, I discount, writing against their name:
'Has not won a handicap this season: can be discounted.' Up to the beginning of June, if they can not be eliminated on other grounds, they are marked down as: 'can not be discounted.'

**Has not won on this type of course**. What is to be done if a horse has only won on a certain type of course (flat or uphill finish)?
If this preference is marked, i.e. the horse has won four or more races only on a certain type of course, and if it is running on a different type of course, it should be discounted.
When there is no marked preference, because the horse has won fewer than four races, then your decision depends on whether it is a winner on flat courses, or on those with an uphill finish. If it has only won on flat courses, it should be discounted when running at a course with an uphill finish. If it has won on an uphill finish course, but not on a flat course, then in my experience, it is best to put it in the 'can not be discounted' category.

**Held by the Handicapper**. In this case, a horse has run at a course and distance reasonably similar to that of today's race, and been unable to win. Whether he ran well or badly, if he is still on the same mark, it is reasonable to assume that he is held by the Handicapper and he can safely be discounted. He can be discounted even more safely, if, however well he runs, he has not succeeded in winning, and the Handicapper has raised his mark.

**Too high in the weights**. Any horse which is carrying more than 10st.

Having discounted all bar two or at most three of the runners, apart from the course and distance winners, you will then be left with a number of horses whose chances can not be discounted. Essentially, these will all be distance winners at similar courses.
The other category which you can not discount is 'dark horses'. These are lightly-raced horses which have won a handicap over the distance, but which may not have won for some time. This is the only point in this system where you even need to look at the trainers' names on the racecard, to see whether this is one of the handful of trainers (e.g. Reg Akehurst, John Dunlop, John Gosden, Lynda Ramsden, Mick Ryan, Michael Stoute) whose 'dark horses' stand a good chance of winning.
You will be reassured to know that at most there are only four or five 'dark horses' per season. In 1995, there were four: POLO KIT (Race 661 18 April Newmarket - a loser); HAZARD A GUESS (Race 841 1 May Pontefract - a winner); KNAVE'S ASH (Race 1179 20 May Thirsk - a loser); and STEVIE'S WONDER (Race 1844 20 June Thirsk - a loser). Although they are not selections, these 'dark horses' can not be discounted.
So now you have a list of horses which are marked as: 'can not be discounted' or 'dark horses'. These are the horses which I regard as the challengers to my selection. Surprisingly enough, there are very few races in which there are more than three challengers to my selection (in 1995, there were none).
Every factor analysed so far has had a bearing on the chances of particular horses.

# How to Beat the Handicapper

But are there any characteristics of a race *as a whole*, which suggest that it is more likely to give a predictable result, or that it should be avoided? I have looked at two such characteristics: the structure, and the competitiveness of a handicap.

I owe the idea of the structure of the handicap to a correspondent to *Raceform Update*, Eric Bowers. He argues that it is possible to assess a handicap by examining its structure. If I understand Mr. Bowers correctly, the following is what he calls an example of an *evenly* balanced handicap:

8 September DONCASTER (Race 3597 DONCASTER Good to soft)

| ANN'S PEARL | 4-10-0 |
| BEAU VENTURE | 7-9-13 |
| POLLY PARTICULAR | 3-9-12 |
| BROADSTAIRS BEAUTY | 5-9-11 |
| THICK AS THIEVES | 3-9-10 |
| LADY SHERIFF | 4-9-10 |
| HERE COMES A STAR | 7-9-8 |
| SHADOW JURY | 5-9-7 |
| SOUND THE TRUMPET | 3-9-7 |
| BOLD STREET | 5-9-6 |
| GENERAL SIR PETER | 3-9-5 |
| BOLLIN HARRY | 3-9-3 |
| NITE-OWL DANCER | 3-9-3 |
| JUST BOB | 6-9-2 |
| JUST DISSIDENT | 3-9-1 |
| CAPTAIN CARAT | 4-9-0 |
| KUNG FRODE | 3-8-12 |

17 runners

In this handicap, the weight range extends from 10st to 8st 12lb, i.e. 16lb. Therefore, the mid point of the handicap is 8lb below the top weight, i.e. 9 st 6lb. If we divide the handicap into those runners above and those below the mid point, we get the following structure:

8 September DONCASTER (Race 3597 DONCASTER Good to soft)

| ANN'S PEARL | 4-10-0 |
| BEAU VENTURE | 7-9-13 |
| POLLY PARTICULAR | 3-9-12 |
| BROADSTAIRS BEAUTY | 5-9-11 |
| THICK AS THIEVES | 3-9-10 |
| LADY SHERIFF | 4-9-10 |
| HERE COMES A STAR | 7-9-8 |
| SHADOW JURY | 5-9-7 |
| SOUND THE TRUMPET | 3-9-7 |
| | |
| MID POINT | 9-6 |
| | |
| BOLD STREET | 5-9-6 |
| GENERAL SIR PETER | 3-9-5 |
| BOLLIN HARRY | 3-9-3 |
| NITE-OWL DANCER | 3-9-3 |
| JUST BOB | 6-9-2 |
| JUST DISSIDENT | 3-9-1 |
| CAPTAIN CARAT | 4-9-0 |
| KUNG FRODE | 3-8-12 |

17 runners

# How to Beat the Handicapper

There are 9 runners above the mid point, and 8 on or below it, so this can be considered a balanced handicap, but some races may be *balanced below the mid-point of the handicap*. For example:

28 October NEWMARKET (Race 4267 1m Good to firm)

| | |
|---|---|
| KAYVEE | 6-10-0 |
| NIGHT DANCE | 3-9-7 |
| TARAWA | 3-9-2 |
| WEAVER BIRD | 5-9-2 |
| SHARP REVIEW | 7-9-2 |
| | |
| MID POINT | 9-2 |
| | |
| WESTERN FAME | 3-9-1 |
| RON'S SECRET | 3-9-1 |
| ETHBAAT | 4-9-1 |
| DELTA SOLEIL | 3-8-13 |
| BILLY BUSHWACKER | 4-8-13 |
| STONE RIDGE | 3-8-13 |
| WAKEEL | 3-8-12 |
| COMANCHE COMPANION | 5-8-11 |
| BALL GOWN | 5-8-10 |
| ERTLON | 5-8-10 |
| COOL EDGE | 4-8-9 |
| MO-ADDAB | 5-8-9 |
| OUR RITA | 6-8-9 |
| CELESTIAL CHOIR | 5-8-9 |
| SERIOUS | 5-8-8 |
| PAY HOMAGE | 7-8-8 |
| COUNTRY LOVER | 4-8-7 |
| CONSPICUOUS | 5-8-7 |
| CLIFTON FOX | 3-8-6 |
| SAMBA SHARPLY | 4-8-5 |
| CELTIC FRINGE | 3-8-5 |
| NOBLE SPRINTER | 3-8-5 |
| MA PETITE ANGLAISE | 3-8-4 |
| APOLLONO | 3-8-4 |
| SAIFAN | 6-8-4 |

30 runners

Here there are 25 runners below the mid-point, and only 5 above it.

Others may be *balanced towards the top of the handicap*, as in the following example.

26 August NEWCASTLE (Race 3368 1m Good to firm)

| | |
|---|---|
| HAKIKA | 3-10-0 |
| CRUMPTON HILL | 3-10-0 |
| CLIFTON FOX | 3-9-12 |
| DESERT TIME | 5-9-12 |
| KEMO SABO | 3-9-9 |
| ALMOND ROCK | 3-9-7 |
| CURRENT SPEECH | 4-9-7 |
| SHINEROLLA | 3-9-5 |
| FOREVER DIAMONDS | 8-9-5 |

# How to Beat the Handicapper

| | |
|---|---|
| MID POINT | 8-11 |
| SCARABEN | 7-8-11 |
| THATCHED | 5-8-4 |
| MARY'S CASE | 5-8-2 |
| MAROWINS | 6-7-8 |

13 runners

In this case, there are 4 runners at or below the mid-point, and 9 above it.

This is an idea worth exploring, as it does show up the peculiar structure of some handicaps, and may explain results which are so far difficult to understand. To date, I have not analysed enough examples in each category to be able to state conclusively that you should select or avoid handicaps with a certain type of structure. So that you can draw your own conclusions, I have given the weights for every race analysed in chapter 5.

While I have still to come to a conclusion about the *structure* of handicaps, my analysis of the *competitiveness* of handicaps gives very clear results.

I judge the competitiveness of a handicap not by the number of handicap winners, nor by the number of distance or course and distance winners, nor by the mark allocated to the top weight, but by the number of challengers there are to my selection. A challenger is identified by the system's method of weighing up the opposition, as set out on the previous pages. In my view, these are the only horses which have a worthwhile chance.

Using this criterion, how competitive are the handicaps which I have assessed? Does betting only in less-competitive handicaps give more profitable results?

In 1995, the answer to the first question is much the same as in other seasons. The majority of handicaps were rather uncompetitive, as can be seen from the table:

| NUMBER OF CHALLENGERS | PERCENTAGE OF RACES * |
|---|---|
| None | 63% |
| One | 18% |
| Two or more | 18% |

* (This table analyses only those races in which there was a selection)

The answer to the second question tends to vary from season to season, and the distribution of betting patterns. For 1995, the answer was:

| NUMBER OF CHALLENGERS | STRIKE-RATE * |
|---|---|
| None | 66% |
| One | 28% |
| Two or more | 28% |

* (This table analyses only those races in which there was a selection)

This is an atypical distribution of strike-rates. Over a longer period, the gap between the strike-rate for 'no challengers' and 'one challenger' is much closer.

In 1995 there were only seven races with two or more challengers, so the figure given above is rather misleading. Over a longer period, the results are much more encouraging, with a strike-rate in such races of around 35%. To complicate matters still further, the average winning price of this type of race is more than high enough to compensate for the relatively low strike-rate.

The only conclusions which can be drawn from this rather complicated picture are that if you are risk-averse in terms of strike-rate, it is better to concentrate on races with no or only one challenger; whereas if you are a risk-taker, and can stand the longer losing runs, the two challenger races are rewarding enough.

This completes the explanation of how to assess both course and distance winners, and the opposition, i.e. the other distance winners. If the system seems to be rather complicated, remember that 90% of the system is entirely methodical, and does not require logic or intuition. To reassure yourself that this is essentially a simple method, take a look at a race with no course and distance winners.

### Abbreviations

| | |
|---|---|
| C/D | = has won a handicap over the course and distance * |
| D | = has won a handicap over the distance * |
| H | = has won a handicap, but not over the distance |
| NWH | = has not won a handicap on the Flat (excluding All-Weather) |
| NWR | = has not won a race on the Flat (excluding All-Weather) |

* In the sporting press, you will notice horses which are marked as 'CD'. This does not necessarily mean that they have won a *handicap* over the course and distance. Likewise, a horse may be marked as 'D' in the press, without necessarily having won a *handicap* over the distance.

28 October NEWMARKET (Race 4268 7f Good to firm)

| | | | |
|---|---|---|---|
| 243101 | QUILLING | 3-10-0 | D |
| 200131 | NIGHT WINK | 3-9-12 | H |
| -00011 | OARE SPARROW | 5-9-10 | H |
| 050050 | THATCHERELLA | 4-9-10 | H |
| 1U0030 | MOUNTGATE | 3-9-7 | H |
| 0-00001 | EUPHYLLIA | 3-9-5 | NWH |
| -05304 | ZELDA ZONK | 3-9-3 | NWR |
| 40000/ | JAHANGIR | 6-9-2 | H |
| 000100 | THUNDER RIVER | 5-9-2 | D |
| 420430 | WINSOME WOOSTER | 4-9-2 | H |
| 042115 | CRETAN GIFT | 4-9-0 | NWH |
| 30-6000 | ROYAL CARLTON | 3-8-13 | NWR |
| 630500 | CANARY FALCON | 4-8-12 | NWH |
| 303040 | LOUISVILLE BELLE | 6-8-6 | H |
| 300200 | SPECTACLE JIM | 6-8-1 | H |
| 000340 | RACING TELEGRAPH | 5-7-9 | NWH |

16 runners

### Distance winners

QUILLING 10/95 Redcar 7f. Won two races over 7f at Redcar.

THUNDER RIVER 9/95 Yarmouth apprentice. In last race, beaten over 7f at Newbury, 19 October 1995.

### Handicap winners

JAHANGIR 8/93 Carlisle 1m. Not won since 1993.

# How to Beat the Handicapper

LOUISVILLE BELLE 6/95 Windsor 6f. Not won since this race; running over 5f and 6f.

MOUNTGATE 7/95 Beverley 7f 100y. Has subsequently run over 7f, without winning.

NIGHT WINK 10/95 Redcar 1m. Won quite well last time out at Redcar.

OARE SPARROW 9/95 Folkestone 6f.

SPECTACLE JIM 7/93 Windsor 6f. Not won since 1993.

THATCHERELLA 5/95 Chepstow 6f. Not won since this race; running over 5f and 6f.

WINSOME WOOSTER 9/94 Bath 5f 161y. Not won this season.

The two distance winners (QUILLING, THUNDER RIVER) have won at flat, easy courses (Redcar, Yarmouth) which are nothing like Newmarket. Of these two, QUILLING is in good form, but it is sheer guesswork to know whether he can win here.

The eight handicap winners have won at a variety of distances. Of these, five (LOUISVILLE BELLE, OARE SPARROW, SPECTACLE JIM, THATCHERELLA, WINSOME WOOSTER) have only won at sprint distances, and it seems like end-of-season desperation to try them over 7f.

Two (JAHANGIR, NIGHT WINK) have won over 1m, but only NIGHT WINK has recent form. But as he has been put back in distance since this race, he would be a false-priced favourite (see chapter 4). The reason for making him a favourite would be that he could win over a shorter trip at a much more testing course. The remaining horse (MOUNTGATE) has won over a stiff course (Beverley), but at a slightly longer distance. He has failed twice over the present distance.

Look through this race, and see how much agonising you would undergo if you tried to make a selection! Horses are running at the 'wrong' distance, or the 'wrong' course, or have no recent form at all.

The betting did favour NIGHT WINK, at 9-4. In such an imponderable 16-runner handicap, this was very poor value, and it is annoying that there was no clear-cut selection in this race. MOUNTGATE (14-1) won quite well, beating QUILLING (10-1) into second place.

The next chapter shows how to profit from the infinitely more clear-cut method of concentrating only on course and distance winners, by using an equally methodical approach to betting.

## SUMMARY

### 1. Identifying a course and distance qualifier

Has it won a handicap over today's course and distance?

Was it a 'proper' handicap, i.e. not an amateur, apprentice, claiming, or selling handicap?

Was its most recent win at the same distance?

Did it record its course and distance win with an acceptable style?

If the answer is 'no' to any of these questions, look at another race. If the answer is 'yes' to all of them, then move on to the next step.

# How to Beat the Handicapper

## 2. Checking the qualifier's form credentials

The correct answers are given in bold type.

Recent form: early season. Did it either win the same race in the previous season, off the same or a lower mark or win over course and distance in October or November of the previous season? **Yes**.

Recent form: the main season. Has it won a handicap this season? **Yes**.

Recent form: up to ninety days. Has it won within the last ninety days? **Yes**.

Is it suited by the going? **Yes**.

Is it held by the Handicapper? **No**.

Was it heavily punished by the Handicapper for its win last time out? **No**.

Is it too high in the handicap? **No**.

Is it too high in the weights? **No**.

Is it ridden by a 5lb or 7lb claimer? **No**.

Has it only won against fillies and mares? **No**.

If all the answers match those given above, then the candidate is a selection.

## 3. Weighing up the opposition.

If it has not won a race or a handicap, discount.

If it has won a handicap over the distance, follow the same procedure as above, steps 2 (Checking the qualifier's form credentials) and 3 (Weighing up the opposition).

If it passes all the tests in steps 2 and 3, then it can not be discounted, and you must ask the extra question:

Is it suited by the course?

If the answer is 'yes', then this is an opponent which can not be discounted; if the answer is 'no', then it can safely be discounted.

# CHAPTER FOUR

# LOSING FAVOURITES

In this system, the overall strike-rate is usually around 50%, so you must expect some losing runs of four or five. To carry you through these losing runs, you need a sound betting strategy. The simplest of staking systems, a level-stake bet on every selection, has much to recommend it: it is simple to operate, and it prevents you increasing stakes after a loser.

However, in a losing run of five or more, your losses begin to run away with you, so I recommend that you adopt the 10% system. Set aside as a bank a sum which you are prepared to lose in full. Your first bet is 10% of your bank. Then you add the profits or subtract the losses from this bet to make a new bank, and for you second bet, the stake is 10% of the new bank. Repeat the process with every new bet. This is the best simple system for following the basic principle of playing up your winnings and cutting your losses.

The latter is more important, as it keeps you in the game during a run of misfortune. See how it compares with a level stakes system. Say that your bank is £1000, and your level-stakes bet is 10% of the bank, i.e. £100 each bet. After five losers, you will have lost £500, while after five losers following the 10% staking system, you will have lost £410. After six losers, the respective amounts are £600 and £470. After ten losers, you will be completely wiped out using level stakes, while on the 10% system you will have £350 left.

The second factor in making this (or, for that matter, any other) system profitable is getting value in each particular bet. If you have selected a course and distance winner, often with good recent form, and known to act on the going, surely this is such a 'stand-out' selection that it will certainly be a short-priced favourite? How can you expect to get the improbable combination of strong form and long price?

In fact, this is a definite example of finding out that how horses perform is not as surprising as how punters think they are going to perform! In 1995, the selections listed at the end of chapter 5 were favourites in 13/38 races (i.e. 34% of the races). Of these, 6/13 won, i.e. 46%, a strike-rate which is below the strike-rate of 56% for selections which are *not* favourite (14/25). This is a slightly unusual result: over a number of seasons, the strike-rate of selections when favourites tends to be about the same (rather than lower, as in 1995) as the strike-rate for selections which are not favourite.

Given the much shorter prices you get when backing favourites, you could simply decide not to back a selection when it is a favourite. This will give you a much better return for your money.

Betting against the favourite has a lot to recommend it in any case. Look at the record of winning favourites in handicap races at selected courses (figures up to the end of the 1995 Flat):

| | | |
|---|---|---|
| Ascot | 3 y o | 16.1% |
| Ascot | all-aged | 16.8% |
| Bath | 3 y o | 36.9% |
| Bath | all-aged | 23.6% |
| Beverley | 3 y o | 20.2% |
| Beverley | all-aged | 27.5% |
| Doncaster | 3 y o | 25.2% |
| Doncaster | all-aged | 23.5% |
| Haydock | 3 y o | 21.6% |

# How to Beat the Handicapper

| | | |
|---|---|---|
| Haydock | all-aged | 19.9% |
| Leicester | 3 y o | 25.0% |
| Leicester | all-aged | 14.2% |
| Newcastle | 3 y o | 34.5% |
| Newcastle | all-aged | 28.5% |
| Newmarket (Rowley) | 3 y o | 15.2% |
| Newmarket (Rowley) | all-aged | 19.2% |
| Pontefract | 3 y o | 31.9% |
| Pontefract | all-aged | 23.5% |

Given a 20% chance of winning, a favourite has to be at 4-1 just to break even over a series of bets. The approximate figures for the 'break-even' prices are:

| | |
|---|---|
| 15% | 11-2 |
| 20% | 4-1 |
| 25% | 3-1 |
| 30% | 5-2 |
| 35% | 2-1 |

You could adopt a simple system of either betting against the favourite or betting against the favourite when its price would not make it 'break even'. For example, a favourite in an all-aged handicap at Haydock priced at 3-1 is below the 'break-even' point of 4-1, and therefore is at a false price and represents poor value.

However, there is an even more rewarding way of betting against the favourite. It is to identify *false-priced favourites*. If you only bet in races where your past research tells you that the favourite has only a 5% chance of winning, then you score a double hit: the favourite's price is way below its value; and its low price has distorted the market in favour of other runners.

So the key to making any system really profitable is only to bet when there is value in the field, i.e. when you think that the favourite is over-priced. In other words, it is just as important to know how to pick losers as it is to pick winners. This must be the first racing book which tells you how to pick losers as systematically as you identify winners!

However, do not be tempted to identify false-priced favourites and look for a selection. It is true that a race with such a favourite gives you a wide margin of error. If you are a risk lover, this is the type of race to pick; but if you are risk averse, it is much more logical to make a selection before looking for a false-priced favourite than the other way round.

I will now look at these categories, which follow a long-term trend; and I will also show why, on every particular occasion when a favourite falls into this category, there is always a plausible reason why it should do so. With every false-priced favourite, there are always 'good' reasons for suggesting that this particular case can buck the trend - but in the (not very) long term, the trend always prevails.

Selecting false-priced favourites is an entirely mechanical process. There is only one type (Only won over a shorter distance - see below) which requires you to make a judgement, which is not a difficult one.

The categories of false-priced favourite are listed in alphabetical order, not in order of importance or of how often they occur. Some of the examples are taken from races not analysed in chapter 5, because there was no selection in the race.

## ALL-WEATHER FORM
All-Weather racing has been a great boon to backers on the lookout for value in turf racing, as it has provided a fruitful new source of false-priced favourites.

The All-Weather surface is completely different from turf. While it is true that some horses do run well on both surfaces, the form shown on the All-Weather tracks has no bearing whatsoever on the outcome of turf races. A horse which has *only* won an All-Weather handicap, is to be regarded as one which has not won a handicap. Consequently, it is a false-priced favourite. Especially at the beginning of the season, you should watch out for the phrases: 'has been running well on the All-Weather', 'fit from recent outings on the All-Weather.'

KINNEGAD KID had won an All-Weather handicap last time out at Wolverhampton, and was now running on soft going at Leicester (Race 481 30 March 1995). Punters are often tempted to equate the sand surface of the All-Weather with the soft going of the turf, but there really is no comparison. Certainly KINNEGAD KID was very poor value at 9-4 on a turf course where favourites in all-aged handicaps have a winning record of 14%.

## CAN REVERSE THE FORM
There are two slightly different types here.

In a 6f handicap, A beats B by one length, and is raised 3lb by the Handicapper, while B's mark remains unchanged. In a roughly equivalent race, they meet again. The newspaper comment is: 'B can beat A at the revised weights'.

In the second type, A beat B by one length, but this time the Handicapper raises A's mark by 6lb, and reduces B's by 1lb. When they meet again, the newspaper comment is: 'B can make the most of the pull in the weights to reverse the form.'

Both comments seem plausible - yet past analysis has shown that B has only a 5% chance of turning the tables to beat A in a subsequent race, however well B ran in the previous race. The explanation may be that in this case weight is not as important in the handicapping system as is usually supposed; or that the jockey riding B may feel that he is at a disadvantage given that A won last time.

If this is so, why should newspaper comment consistently favour B to beat A? The answer to this question is the same as that for all types of false-priced favourites: it makes better copy. How much more interesting it is to read: 'B has every chance of beating A at the revised weights, as he was running on well at. the finish in their previous encounter' as compared to 'A has a 95% chance of beating B again.' The latter makes horse-racing seem a very dull, unromantic affair.

This type of false-priced favourite is the best from our point of view, as it has the lowest winning strike-rate. It was a pity that there were no selection races in 1995 in which this type occurred.

The best example in 1995 was from a race in which the race-reader's comment suggested that the second was very unlikely to turn the tables on the first if they met again - yet the second was still made favourite next time out!

In a 7f handicap at Redcar (Race 3980 3 October), QUILLING made all to win 'convincingly' (*Raceform Update*), while the second, MISTER WESTSOUND, receiving 6lb from the winner, was beaten one and three-quarter lengths, was 'hard ridden and ((did)) not run on.' *Raceform Form-Book* noted: 'Should Dettori ride him again, he will surely have learnt something here.'

Next time they met, it was over the same course, distance and going (Race 4236 24 October). QUILLING's mark was now 10lb above that of MISTER WESTSOUND, but he had to concede 17lb in weight, because the latter was ridden, not by Dettori, but by a 7lb claimer. MISTER WESTSOUND was backed down from 8-1 to 9-2 favourite, while QUILLING was well out in the betting at 10-1. This time, MISTER WESTSOUND was beaten even more emphatically, by just under four lengths.

It is rather paradoxical that the only racing cliché apart from 'horses for courses' which has a sound statistical justification, namely 'A horse can give away weight but not distance', is precisely the one which is ignored by punters when making certain horses favourites. Faced with the same opponents, an increase in weight does not as a rule make much difference, if the other conditions (course, distance and going) are the same, or even roughly similar.

## DEFINITELY HELD BY THE HANDICAPPER

This is not a very common category, as you have to be absolutely convinced that the Handicapper has taken the measure of a horse over a suitable course, going and distance.

The best example in 1995 was in Race 3368, an 1m handicap at Newcastle. After winning quite well at Salisbury over 1m, ALMOND ROCK seemed to be unlucky in his next race, over the same course and distance. According to the reports, he had been denied a clear run over one furlong out, and had been beaten three-quarters of a length.

On a course like Salisbury, I am very sceptical about 'hard luck' stories. If the Handicapper had left ALMOND ROCK on the same mark, it would have been a difficult decision, but the fact that he had been raised 2lb made up my mind - he was now definitely held by the Handicapper. The winner, FIONN DE COOL, had not previously won a race.

*Sporting Life* commented: 'ALMOND ROCK's close second to Fionn de Cool last time out suggests she is (reporters are always confused about sex - in fact it is a 'he') not handicapped out of it yet.' I wonder if *'Man on the Spot'* had looked at the handicap marks? In fact, ALMOND ROCK did win again - but not as a favourite.

## NOT WON A FLAT HANDICAP

Even if a horse wins a conditions race very impressively, it enters a different world when running in a handicap. In non-handicaps, many of the runners have little chance, and have no weight advantage as a compensation. On its first run in a handicap, the stakes winner finds no respite: the weaker horses use their pull in the weights to set a good pace from the start, and the rest of the field is often quite closely bunched for most of the trip.

With certain trainers this is a common source of false-priced favourites. Such horses win a maiden race easily or even impressively, and are then entered in a handicap. In British racing, the only possible exception to this rule is John Gosden; and a definite exception in Ireland is Dermot Weld.

Note that 'winning a handicap' is restricted to turf Flat races only. All-Weather racing is quite a different matter: many successful handicap winners on the All-Weather are quite unable to make the transition to racing on turf. They certainly do not have a favourite's chance.

Of course, some handicaps are won by horses which have not won a handicap before, otherwise there would never be any handicap winners - but they do not have a favourite's chance to do so.

Non-winners of handicaps usually make a good story, and there was a really compelling yarn about TOP CEES (Race 661 18 April Newmarket). In 1994 he had run in five handicaps for Peter Harris, over 1m 4f and 1m 5f. Subsequently he had been gelded, and was now trained by Lynda Ramsden. On his only race this season, a 1m 4f apprentice handicap, he had been noted as 'staying on well.' Ignoring the fact that he had yet to win a handicap, the *Sporting Life* commented: 'Ramsden's runners do well here.' In controversial circumstances, he won his next handicap when he was not favourite - but he certainly was not a 5-1 favourite to win here.

## NOT WON A FLAT HANDICAP THIS SEASON

This applies only after the beginning of June, as up to that point winners from previous seasons can win again before the competition hots up. Thereafter, a horse without a win in a handicap, and not just a race (even if it is a Group race), does not have a favourite's chance.

In SEA-DEER's last victory (Race 2584 27 July 1994 Goodwood) he had been ridden out to win over 5f, running off a mark of 79. In his final race of the previous season, also over 5f (race 3628 23 September 1994 Ascot), and running of a mark of 89, he had run on to be beaten one length. For this performance, he had been raised 1lb, to 90. In 1995, he had run twice before this race: over 6f at Newbury, 'backward, ran on inside final furlong' beaten four lengths (Race 1174 20 May 1995); and over 6f at Kempton (Race 1316 Kempton 27 May 1995), beaten four lengths, 'bit backward, never placed to challenge'. On both occasions, he was on a mark of 90, which remained unchanged for this race. Making him 11-2 favourite in the Goodwood race was taking a lot on trust, as he had not won this season and was now on a mark 11lb higher than that of his last victory.

But even when a horse's rating falls, if he has not won this season he does not have a favourite's chance. Since losing his first race right at the beginning of the season, MASTER BEVELED had fallen 13lb in the handicap, to compensate for losing his next seven races. Last time out he had run a respectable fifth, but at this stage of the season (9 September) he did not merit being 4-1 favourite in a big field of handicappers. Probably the reason for favouritism was: 'ran well last time out, and is now on a handy mark' or perhaps 'shows his best form in the autumn'.

MASTER BEVELED ran four more races in 1995 without winning, even being made joint favourite on one occasion. Clearly the Handicapper had him well under control.

In this connection, the phrase to look and listen out for is: 'his turn is near.' Look at a 5f handicap at Ayr, on 14 September 1995 (Race 3667), in which LEPINE was made clear favourite, admittedly at 7-1, in a field of 29 runners. In 1994, he had won two 6f handicaps, at Thirsk (Race 1594 14 June 1994) and Ripon (Race 2069 4 July 1994), but did not win again, finishing on a handicap mark of 76. In 1995, he had run honestly, being placed in six of his seven races before going to Ayr. On his previous outing (Race 3279 23 August Ascot 5f), he had finished five lengths third, off the same mark (74). There was no doubt about his performance: *Raceform* commented that he was 'unable to quicken' and was 'tapped for toe.'

Sympathising with his very able trainer, punters hoped that 'his turn was near', as he had been placed in most of his races, and was on a reasonable handicap mark. Yet he had not won at all this season, and there was no reason why he should, especially at a shorter distance than that over which he had gained his only two wins. Racing does not operate on the 'Buggins turn' principle, where long and honest service is eventually rewarded. However sympathetic you may feel towards his owner and trainer, the race is to the swift.

It might be worth keeping a list of horses *not* to follow: on his only other race in 1995 (Race 4113 14 October Catterick 5f), he was made 11-2 joint favourite. Again, he gave of his best, but made no impression.

## NOT WON A FLAT RACE

This falls into the 'incredible but true' category. Horses of this type are the 'poor bloody infantry' of racing: in the races analysed in this book, they made up 13.4% of the runners, but only 2.2% of the winners, about par for the course.

Could there ever be a favourite to win a handicap which had never won a Flat race? It is hard to believe, but this does happen, admittedly only once or twice a season. In 1995, DANCING DESTINY (Race 1658 12 June Warwick) was made 15-8 clear favourite, even though she had been beaten eight lengths in a maiden stakes. Usually this type of favourite has run 'well' enough (without winning) in an All-Weather race to 'suggest' that she might be suited by the turf, but she finished a well-beaten seventh.

# How to Beat the Handicapper

## NOT WON A RACE FOR AT LEAST ONE SEASON

A horse which has not won for at least one season is very much an unknown quantity. It may (at last! says the trainer) have come down to the handicap mark from which it last won, after races at the 'wrong' course and distance. But do not imagine that even the trainer can be 100% confident that it can win again off its suitable mark - there is a world of difference between a promising gallop at home, and the much more competitive world of the racecourse. At least the trainer knows that the horse is fit, whereas unless you have stable information, you do not even know whether he is ready to run or not.

Alternatively, it may have shown very good form two or more seasons ago, and then been absent due to injury. It is equally difficult to say whether it has retained its form.

But a horse returning from injury is a real *Boys' Own* story. One of the best in 1995 concerned TAMARPOUR (Race 1444 2 June Bath 2m 1f 34y). He had not won since June 1991, four years ago almost to the day, yet he was at times the clear market leader, and ended up the joint 4-1 favourite. Could Martin Pipe work a miracle? If he could, he was taking no chances. TAMARPOUR appeared wearing bandages on his near foreleg, which strongly suggested that he had not made a full recovery from injury.

## NOT WON ON THE GOING

Where a runner has not won on today's going, or has shown a marked preference for a different type of going, or is unproven on today's going, it seems unwise to make him the favourite.

In a 6f handicap at Ripon (Race 1414 31 May 1995), the inappropriately-named SHOWERY had won only one race, on good going, and was now being tried over good to firm. Very few fillies and mares have a preference for such fast going, but if she had a proven record on such going, that would have been acceptable. In the circumstances, to make her 6-5 favourite seemed hard to understand until you read the press comment: won easily, now on the same handicap mark because the previous race was for apprentices, and her apprentice can now claim 5lb against the other jockeys.

Reading the race reports, I noticed that she had worn a bandage on her hind legs, which suggested that her trainer (Bill Watts) may have feared that she would be injured on the harder ground.

## ONLY WON OVER A SHORTER DISTANCE

This is the only type of false-priced favourite where judgement is required. When a winner is put over a longer distance than that of his previous wins, you may consider that there is nothing in his previous form which justifies making him favourite.

The press comment may be that 'his style of racing suggests that he would be suited by a longer distance' or 'stoutly bred on his dam's side, he is sure to get further.' This is guesswork, certainly in handicap racing. If the record shows that he has a marked preference for the shorter distance, and that the race readers' comments are not encouraging, then he is a false-priced favourite.

Here is a typical example, from a race in which there was a selection. SWEET MAGIC had only won one handicap, over 5f at Sandown in July 1994 (Race 2288), being noted as 'hard ridden and led last stride.' In his only other race thereafter, a 5f handicap at Goodwood (Race 2599) he had been beaten a neck: 'every chance final two furlongs, ran on'.

But given his record to date, it was difficult to see how in a race over 6f at Goodwood (Race 1241 24 May) he could be made a 9-4 favourite, especially when faced with a tried and tested 6f performer (and course and distance winner) CASTLEREA LAD.

If the race-reader's comments had been: 'running on well in the closing stages' or 'staying on well', you might have thought that it was worthwhile trying him over 6f. In that case, although he would not be regarded as a challenger to the selection, since he had not won over the distance, he could not be considered as a false-priced favourite either.

## PUT BACK IN DISTANCE

This is rather like 'can reverse the form', a racing cliché with little validity. It applies both to horses which have never won over the distance, and to horses which have won over the distance, then won over a longer distance, and in this race are put back to the original winning distance.

It is quite different from 'only won over a shorter distance'. In some cases, horses winning over a shorter distance can be regarded as having a reasonable chance when tackling a longer trip for the first time; but, in my view, there are no circumstances when a horse set to run over a shorter distance has a worthwhile chance.

What both types do have in common, is that the racing press has a fixed idea about the best distance for a horse, and re-cycles the story even when the facts are against it.

In 1995, a good example was CAPTAIN CARAT. Before running over 5f at Doncaster (Race 3597 8 September 1995), CAPTAIN CARAT had won twice over six furlongs at Doncaster. For his connections, he must have been a very frustrating horse. After winning reasonably well over the course and distance on 8 May 1995, off 59, he had been placed several times when running off a mark of 64 or 65. I don't think that the trainer, Mrs. Ramsden, is always a good judge of the right distance for a horse, but in this case, it seemed reasonable to try a different distance, since clearly he was held off 65 (today's mark) at 6f.

But in these circumstances he was not a reasonable favourite at 3-1. The *Sporting Life*'s comment was a classic: CAPTAIN CARAT had run well over 5f, 'admittedly on heavy going', and he 'likes Doncaster'. In the event, he ran well enough ('hampered over one furlong out, stayed on strongly towards the finish', beaten one length) to encourage his supporters to make him favourite again, on 21 September 1995 at Pontefract (Race 3783), at an even shorter price, 9-4. Again he failed to get a clear run, and was beaten by about the same distance.

CAPTAIN CARAT is one type: the distance is different, but the course conformation is the same. There is an apparently more plausible case: the distance is shorter, but the course is more testing. Look at the example of DOUBLE BOUNCE in a 5f handicap at Sandown (Race 3219 18 August 1995). *Sporting Life* argued that: '...he is effective over 5f and the stiff nature of this course will suit him.' His past handicap record was two wins over 6f, at Folkestone and Nottingham. Last time out, he ran on well near the finish at Salisbury, over 6f. There was also a plausible story line.

In 1994 he had been trained by the highly competent Ken Ivory, but had now been transferred to the equally capable Peter Makin. But a horse's chances would have to be rated much more than plausible to be worth backing at 15-8 in a Sandown sprint handicap!

This completes the list of categories of false-priced favourite. Sometimes you find a horse which falls into more than one of the categories. Take, for example, the 5f handicap at Thirsk on 5 June 1995 (Race 1508). SUPERPRIDE had not won a handicap, not won on the going (good to firm) and was backed to reverse the form with LADY SHERIFF. For good measure, the only race he had won (Race 1667 18 June 1994) was over a longer distance (6f)!

Even if there is a false-priced favourite, the price of the selection may still be too low to make it worthwhile having a bet. There were two examples in 1994. OBELOS (Race 841 26 April Catterick 1m 3f 214y) a loser, and SPECIAL DAWN (Race 1753

# How to Beat the Handicapper

Sandown 1m 2f 7y), a winner. Both were at 9-4.

At this point, the reader may be wondering: I can see that there is no form justification for these horses being made favourite, and I accept that favourites in these categories do have a very low strike-rate. But surely such false-priced favourites do not occur very often? Surprisingly, they do. In 1995, 47% (18/38) of the races analysed in this book (selections only) included a false-priced favourite. This is not an exceptional result, being only slightly below the long-term trend of 49%.

I do not know how frequently false-priced favourites occur in handicaps not analysed for the purposes of this system. Even if there were significantly fewer (say one in three of all handicap races) this would still mean that on average there would be at least one false-priced favourite every racing day. If you wanted to have a bet every day, it would make sense to bet only in these races. The only problem would be that, although the press gives a very good guide to likely starting prices, it can not anticipate, e.g. that there will be a weight of money for Dettori to complete the third leg of a treble. The drawback is that this would mean analysing every handicap on a day's programme.

To see how and why such false-priced favourites arise, it is important to understand the betting market. Nowadays, there are very few meetings at which there are individual big bettors, or a stable having a gamble. Most bookmakers, and certainly the big operators, do not have a view on a race. Their aim is to make money over a series of races regardless of their own opinions about the result of any one race. Making a book on the basis of their own opinions would certainly not be approved of by their head offices.

So if you are not betting against big backers, trainers, owners, or bookmakers, in that their views do not determine the prices, who are you betting against?

The answer is: the millions of other betting shop punters. In this set-up, one punter's loss is another punter's gain, and the only long-term winner is the bookmaker. He acts merely as an agent for the whole business of betting to take place, and aims to make a given percentage profit regardless of the results.

If the market is organised in this way, how and why do the types of false-priced favourite identified in this chapter arise? There are two distinct patterns.

Firstly, the bookmakers organise a 'pre-emptive' strike, by making a given horse favourite, using their monetary muscle in the on-course market. For example, because Frankie Dettori has already won two races today, his horse may be made favourite because it carries a weight of betting shop money invested in doubles, trebles, accumulators, and so on. In this case, the price against Dettori's mount in no way represents a reasonable value.

Secondly, most favourites do in fact have a good chance on form, but a significant minority have been made favourite by the betting shop punters, for reasons which do not have much to do with form. The punters' views are both formed by and catered to by the sporting press. In some aspects of their job, racing journalists seem rather lazy - how often do you read a full report of the last race of the day, even when it finishes fairly early? But in respect of providing copy for the features which sum up races in advance, I have no criticism of racing journalists.

Their task has become all the more difficult with the expansion of the racing programme. For six races at every meeting, they must aim to say something interesting and attention-catching. 'Course-and-distance winner can repeat his victory over the second horse' is much less attention-catching than 'Second last time out, he was running on well at the finish after being hampered in the early stages, and can reverse the form given the pull in the weights.'

Some columnists have a great and deserved following among racegoers. For instance, Mark Winstanley of the *Sporting Life* is a brilliant tipster, with an impressive strike-rate. Even allowing for the fact that the publication of his column shortens the prices of his selections, he regularly picks long-priced winners.

Many of his selections seems to be made on the basis of being informed by or second-guessing the intentions of trainers, particularly David Loder or the late Jack Holt, rather than weighing up the horse's chances. On this basis, his selections are a good source of false-priced favourites (though it has to be admitted that he selected the one winning false-priced favourite of 1995, VERZEN, Race 2948 5 August Newmarket).

The important thing to remember is that in every particular case, the story seems highly plausible, and it seems much more exciting to try to buck, rather than follow, a trend. But only about one in twenty of the 'can reverse the form' type of favourite wins, so would you rather be a boring winner than an exciting loser?

So it is easy to explain why the false (short) price for the favourite has also created a false (long) price for your selection. What is not at all easy to explain is that the strike-rate for selections running against a false-priced favourite is higher than the average strike-rate. In 1995, the strike-rate for selections in races where there was a clear false-priced favourite (i.e. not a joint favourite with the selection) was 68%, significantly higher than the overall strike-rate of 53%. This was not an exceptional season, as the average strike-rate for such races is around 65%.

This surprising result has been tested over ten years of selections, and has consistently remained the same.

I am completely at a loss to explain this discrepancy. Logically speaking, it is easy to see that the presence of a false-priced favourite lengthens the price of the selection, but it is not easy to understand why the selection then has a better chance of winning. After all, when you exclude the false-priced favourite from the race, you are not thereby increasing the selection's chances as such. But even if the strike-rate fell to the average for all races, it would still be worth trying to find false-priced favourites, because of the better value you would obtain against your selection.

I would only lose confidence in this result if: the proportion of winning false-priced favourites rose dramatically from its current level of 5%; and if the strike-rate and the price of selections winning such races fell calamitously.

## TYPES OF FALSE-PRICED FAVOURITES

(given in alphabetical order, rather than in order of importance or of how often they occur)

All-Weather form
Can reverse the form
Definitely held by the Handicapper
Not won a Flat handicap
Not won a Flat handicap this season (in a race after Epsom Derby meeting)
Not won a Flat race
Not won for at least one season (in a race before Epsom Derby meeting)
Not won on the going
Only won over a shorter distance
Put back in distance

# CHAPTER FIVE

# AN AVERAGE SEASON: 1995

While this was an average season for course and distance winners, it was exceptional in one respect: the paucity of selections in September and October. I think that this can be accounted for by the fact that the going continued to be good to firm right until the last racing day. It must have been very frustrating for owners and trainers to have hardly any opportunities for the horses which only show their form on good to soft or soft going.

Now to look at the season in detail. All the 38 races in which there were definite selections, and 6 races which did not generate selections, but which illustrated features of the system, are analysed here.

### Notes and abbreviations

1. All-Weather form is given in *italic* type.

2. The race numbers are taken from the official form book, *Raceform*.

3. Very occasionally, the betting shows are not the same as those reported in *Raceform Update*. Instead, I report the betting as I experienced it at the time.

4. No indication is given of the classification of the handicap (e.g. 0-75), since in this system it is immaterial.

| | |
|---|---|
| C/D | = has won a handicap over the course and distance * |
| D | = has won a handicap over the distance * |
| H | = has won a handicap, but not over the distance |
| NWH | = has not won a handicap on the Flat (excluding All-Weather) |
| NWR | = has not won a race on the Flat (excluding All-Weather) |

* In the sporting press, you will notice horses which are marked as 'CD'. This does not necessarily mean that they have won a *handicap* over the course and distance. Likewise, a horse may be marked as 'D' in the press, without necessarily having won a *handicap* over the distance.

The first race of the season, a 23-runner sprint handicap, was a laborious one to unravel, although the result was rewarding. Since it is the first example, I will explain the method of analysis in detail, so that in subsequent examples this will not be necessary.

If you find the process of analysing this particular race rather too complicated for the first example using a new system, look at the next race (Race 661), a much simpler race.

5 April RIPON (Race 535: 6f Good to soft)

| | | | |
|---|---|---|---|
| 014000- | PETE AFRIQUE | 4-10-0 | H |
| 000402- | PALACEGATE TOUCH | 5-9-10 | C/D |
| 140020- | JUST BOB | 6-9-5 | D |
| 00600-1 | CASTLEREA LAD | 6-9-4 | D |
| 15023- | TSHUSICK | 4-9-4 | NWH |
| 0/0000- | TRUTHFUL IMAGE | 6-9-1 | D |

| | | | |
|---|---|---|---|
| 13315- | WHITTLE WOODS GIRL | 4-9-1 | C/D |
| 00010-1 | SADDLEHOME | 6-8-13 | H |
| 10001-2 | SAILORMAITE | 4-8-13 | D |
| 2-56104 | DESERT INVADER | 4-8-10 | H |
| 055000- | SAMSOLOM | 7-8-9 | H |
| 11000-0 | ELLE SHAPED | 5-8-9 | H |
| 00000-0 | BRAILLE | 4-8-8 | NWH |
| 323020- | MAID O'CANNIE | 4-8-8 | NWH |
| 512210- | BELLA PARKES | 4-8-6 | D |
| 00032-0 | CAPTAIN CARAT | 4-8-3 | D |
| 100060- | COLWAY RAKE | 4-8-1 | NWH |
| 0200-45 | PLUM FIRST | 5-7-11 | D |
| 050130- | MU-ARRIK | 7-7-10 | D |
| 065400- | RANKAIDADE | 4-7-10 | NWH |
| 42-2550- | TEE TEE TOO | 3-7-9 | NWH |
| 03404-2 | THE OLD CHAPEL | 6-7-9 | NWH |
| 00-1100 | PINE RIDGE LAD | 5-7-7 | C/D |

23 runners

This race was unusual in that there were two possible selections, and the going would decide which would be adopted.

## C/D winners

PALACEGATE TOUCH same race 1994. After winning this race (Race 456 'held on well') first time out in 1994 off a mark of 88, he lost 11 races, bringing his mark down to 86 for this race. He has a marked preference for good to soft, and if the going became any firmer, he would not be a selection.

PINE RIDGE LAD 7/93. Not won since 1993.

WHITTLE WOODS GIRL 8/94. She won twice over the course and distance in 1994, including the high class Great St. Wilfrid handicap. Her only subsequent race in 1994 was in a very competitive 6f handicap at Ayr, where she was only beaten three heads and 3/4l. However, she had a marked preference for good or good to firm going, although she had won once on soft. If the going firmed up dramatically, she would be preferred over PALACEGATE TOUCH.

## D winners

BELLA PARKES 7/93 Hamilton. Not won since 1993.

CAPTAIN CARAT 7/94 Nottingham. Not won on the going.

CASTLEREA LAD 3/95 Doncaster. Not won on the going.

JUST BOB 4/93 claiming handicap. Not won since 1993.

MU-ARRIK 9/94 Haydock seller. Not won a 'proper' handicap.

PLUM FIRST 6/94 Redcar. Well beaten off 58, now on 59.

SAILORMAITE 10/94 Leicester. Not won on the going.

# How to Beat the Handicapper

TRUTHFUL IMAGE 7/93 Catterick. Not won since 1993.

Selection: PALACEGATE TOUCH (if good to soft, or soft); WHITTLE WOODS GIRL (if good or good to firm).    Challengers: None.

The going was definitely on the soft side of good to soft, so PALACEGATE TOUCH was the selection. As usual, I ignored the effect of the draw, said to favour low numbers in soft going. SAILORMAITE was well held by CASTLEREA LAD on his last outing, so I considered him a false-priced favourite for two reasons: that he could not reverse the form; and that he was unsuited by the going.

PALACEGATE TOUCH managed to edge left from his draw on the far side, and won easily enough in the end, at 9-1. He did not win any of his nine subsequent races in 1995, finishing on a mark of 85. I wonder if a repeat performance in 1996 is on the cards?

18 April NEWMARKET (Race 661 1m 6f Good to firm)

| 40/5523- | NOT IN DOUBT | 6-10-0 | NWH |
| 4601/1-4 | DREAMS END | 7-9-10 | H |
| 0/41250 | SIMAFAR | 4-9-2 | NWH |
| 22311- | TRANS SIBERIA | 4-9-2 | C/D |
| 125112- | WELL BELOVED | 4-9-1 | H |
| 62314-0 | POLO KIT | 4-9-1 | D |
| 11114-0 | CHIMANIMANI | 4-9-0 | H |
| 210100- | RUMI | 4-8-13 | NWH |
| 632215- | TUDOR ISLAND | 6-8-11 | C/D |
| 244012- | THUNDERHEART | 4-8-11 | H |
| 223110- | MICROLITE | 4-8-9 | NWH |
| 56040-6 | TOP CEES | 5-8-9 | NWH |
| 000/ | SWORD MASTER | 6-8-8 | H |
| 210050- | ISLAND BLADE | 6-7-11 | H |
| 4- | HEAD TURNER | 7-7-7 | D |
| 0-05 | GUARDS BRIGADE | 4-7-7 | NWH |

16 runners

It was reassuring the one of the first selections of the season should be at a 'star' course such as Newmarket. Here is the analysis.

## C/D winners

TRANS SIBERIA 10/94 held by TUDOR ISLAND over the course, distance, and going 30 September 1994.

TUDOR ISLAND 9/94. I discounted his only other race thereafter, over 2m at Newbury, 20 October 1994, on good to soft going.

## D winners

HEAD TURNER only won a maiden handicap.

POLO KIT 6/94 Sandown. Beaten over 2m on only subsequent race. A good trainer, so this may be a dark horse.

Selection: TUDOR ISLAND.         Challengers: POLO KIT (dark horse).

# How to Beat the Handicapper

TOP CEES, who had not won a handicap, was the 5-1 favourite. *Sporting Life* commented: 'Ramsden's horses do well here.' The Ramsdens are well known as a betting stable, so journalists found an easy story, and punters tried to second-guess their intentions here. But even if the Ramsdens' intention was to win, TOP CEES had not won a handicap, and so was a false-priced favourite.

Perhaps I was lucky here. With consummate tact, *Raceform* suggested that: ' TOP CEES...was not ridden as though he was well fancied for this. After finding trouble in the last two furlongs, supporters were left wondering what might have been.' TUDOR ISLAND (at 7-1) benefited from TOP CEES' enigmatic performance (an enigma which may have been solved when he gained a 'very smooth success' at Chester on 10 May) by finding just enough to win by one length, from THUNDERHEART.

26 April CATTERICK (Race 757 1m 3f 214y Good)

| | | | |
|---|---|---|---|
| 212600- | GEORGE DILLINGHAM | 5-10-0 | H |
| 5656-00 | SLASHER JACK | 4-9-11 | D |
| 0420-23 | SOUTHERN POWER | 4-9-9 | NWH |
| 13143-1 | COOL LUKE | 6-8-13 | H |
| 431400 | IN THE MONEY | 6-8-5 | D |
| 4440-0 | SALLYOREALLY | 4-8-5 | NWR |
| 04/300 | CHOWPOR | 4-8-4 | NWR |
| 12250-0 | DOUBLE ECHO | 7-8-2 | D |
| 01-1110 | PHARLY DANCER | 6-8-1 | NWH |
| 420532- | SOBA UP | 5-7-8 | H |
| 050640- | KINOKO | 7-7-7 | C/D |
| 65530-1 | MERRY MERMAID | 5-7-7 | D |

12 runners

## C/D winners

KINOKO won this race in 1994, from a mark of 51; in 1993, he had also won in April. Following 7 losing runs in 1994, his mark had been reduced to 48. As a seven-year-old he might not be as good as in the past, but was worth a chance.

## D winners

DOUBLE ECHO 5/94 Newcastle. Held by the Handicapper.

IN THE MONEY 5/94 York. Held by DOUBLE ECHO last time out.

MERRY MERMAID 4/95 Ripon. Had only won a selling handicap.

SLASHER JACK 7/94 York. Only a five-runner race.

Selection: KINOKO.          Challengers: None.

COOL LUKE and DOUBLE ECHO, handicap and distance winners respectively were the joint favourites, with KINOKO at 10-1. Held up in the early stages of the race, he was soon outpaced and never a factor. PHARLY DANCER just got his head in front, to win all out from GEORGE DILLINGHAM.

1 May PONTEFRACT (Race 841 1m 2f 6y Firm)

| | | | |
|---|---|---|---|
| 65-0 | ZARALASKA | 4-10-0 | NWR |

| 21623- | THE LONE DANCER | 4-9-13 | NWH |
|---|---|---|---|
| 005/1 | OBELOS | 4-9-8 | C/D |
| U513-04 | HAZARD A GUESS | 5-9-6 | D |
| 014523 | HILLZAH | 7-9-6 | C/D |
| 000-00 | BRAILLE | 4-9-4 | NWH |
| 221261- | FLOATING LINE | 7-9-2 | H |
| 0/30-56 | ATHERTON GREEN | 5-8-11 | D |
| 05600- | ACCESS CARNIVAL | 4-8-11 | NWR |
| 350004 | SPANISH STRIPPER | 4-8-6 | NWR |
| 0U6060- | BENJAMINS LAW | 4-8-5 | NWR |
| 200310- | DIAMOND CROWN | 4-8-2 | D |
| 040560- | GOLDEN STAR | 4-8-1 | NWR |
| 45365-0 | LOCHORE | 5-8-0 | H |

14 runners

Half the runners in this field had either not won a race or a handicap, making it quite a weak contest.

## C/D winners

HILLZAH 10/94 held by OBELOS last time out.

OBELOS 4/95 was noted by *Reflections on Running* (in *Raceform Update*) as winning decisively, I decided that this outweighed other reports that it had been driven out to win.

## D winners

ATHERTON GREEN 8/93 Newcastle. Had not won since that race.

DIAMOND CROWN 8/94 Nottingham: selling race only.

HAZARD A GUESS 6/94 Sandown. Having won well at Sandown, he had only one further race in 1994, but had shown nothing this season. Very much a dark horse.

<u>Selection</u>: OBELOS.      <u>Challengers</u>: HAZARD A GUESS (dark horse).

OBELOS went off the 9-4 favourite, but ran no sort of race. He dropped away tamely with four furlongs to go, and was virtually tailed off. In the past, he had been very lightly raced because of a tendency to go lame, and it was later reported that this had happened again. HAZARD A GUESS *was* a dark horse, winning comfortably by one length. He also won next time out (at Beverley, on 13 May, in Race 1064), but thereafter the Handicapper had him firmly in his grip.

7 May NEWMARKET (Race 934 6f Good to firm)

| 0550-13 | MONTENDRE | 8-9-7 | NWH |
|---|---|---|---|
| 2116-30 | DOUBLE BLUE | 6-9-5 | C/D |
| 034000- | MASTER PLANNER | 6-8-11 | C/D |
| 50442-6 | LORD OLIVIER | 5-8-10 | NWH |
| 000640- | PINKERTON'S PAL | 4-8-10 | NWH |
| 1500-06 | WELSH MIST | 4-8-9 | H |
| 1450/04 | SNIPE HALL | 4-8-7 | NWH |

| | | | |
|---|---|---|---|
| 12053-6 | ALZIANAH | 4-8-7 | D |
| 36100-1 | DARREN BOY | 4-8-7 | D |
| 3000-21 | DOMULLA | 5-8-7 | D |

10 runners

## C/D winners

DOUBLE BLUE 4/94. Well held by MONTENDRE in a stakes race over the course and distance last time out, at level weights, DOUBLE BLUE seemed a difficult horse to place. His last winning mark in handicaps was 85. Since then he had won Listed races, but had not won any more handicaps. Now his mark was 104, and I thought he was definitely held.

MASTER PLANNER same race 1994. After winning this race off 96, he had run twelve times without success in 1994, so that he was now back to the same mark.

## D winners

ALZIANAH 7/93 Yarmouth. Seemed to have lost her way.

DARREN BOY 7/94 Newmarket July. No form since winning by a neck off 86, now rated 92: definitely held by the Handicapper.

DOMULLA 4/95 Haydock. Only wins on good or good to soft: unsuited by the going.

Selection: MASTER PLANNER.        Challengers: None.

The betting was difficult to weigh up. I could not see DOUBLE BLUE winning this race, but I did not think that he was a false priced favourite either. DOMULLA was an unknown quantity on the going, and on good to firm going definitely not worth being favourite. In the event, they were joint favourites, and MASTER PLANNER went off at 9-1.

MASTER PLANNER beat ALZIANAH by half a length, exactly the same margin as when winning this race in 1994, off the same mark. Horses are not machines? Sometimes I wonder!

12 May BEVERLEY (Race 1036 2m 35y Good to firm)

| | | | |
|---|---|---|---|
| 3422- | HULLBANK | 5-10-0 | NWR |
| 055- | CAVINA | 5-9-1 | NWR |
| 021465- | VAIN PRINCE | 8-8-7 | C/D |
| 4000-21 | ROLLING THE BONES | 6-8-6 | C/D |
| 424606 | MURPHYS WAY | 6-8-5 | NWR |
| 5/060- | BAHRAIN QUEEN | 7-7-8 | NWR |
| 5/0055- | BRUSQUE | 11-7-7 | H |

7 runners

With four of the runners not having won a race, including the top weight, this was about as uncompetitive a race as you could get!

## C/D winners

ROLLING THE BONES same race 1994. Won this race off 35 last year; now running off 41, but clearly in reasonable form, since he won last time out, at Folkestone over 1m 7f 92y.

VAIN PRINCE 8/92 Had run three times since his last victory: held off this mark.

## D winners

None.

## Selection: ROLLING THE BONES. Challengers: None.

In other cases, I have found races which are as weak as this, and have such a 'standout' selection, but still throw up false-priced favourites. Not today, however, as ROLLING THE BONES was a clear favourite at 11-10. Perhaps the only surprising feature of the betting was that GAVINA and HULLBANK were 9-2 joint second favourites, and VAIN PRINCE, the only other distance winner, was 8-1.

The danger of such a weak field is a slow pace, and following a very moderate gallop for over twelve furlongs, ROLLING THE BONES only just got home ahead of VAIN PRINCE.

16 May YORK (Race 1100 6f Good to firm)

| 250-450 | HARD TO FIGURE | 9-9-7 | D |
| 121-304 | BRANSTON ABBY | 6-9-7 | C/D |
| 34000-1 | MASTER PLANNER | 6-9-5 | C/D |
| 00-6414 | VENTURE CAPITALIST | 6-9-3 | D |
| 000540- | ROGER THE BUTLER | 5-9-2 | C/D |
| 531126- | SHEILA'S SECRET | 5-9-1 | H |
| 14351-4 | MONAASSIB | 4-8-13 | NWH |
| 03-006 | CALL ME I'M BLUE | 5-8-12 | H |
| 0442-60 | LORD OLIVIER | 5-8-10 | NWH |
| 450/046 | SNIPE HALL | 4-8-9 | H |
| 0402-15 | PALACEGATE TOUCH | 5-8-9 | D |
| 0400-00 | AMRON | 8-8-9 | H |
| 60000-0 | CELESTIAL KEY | 5-8-7 | NWH |

13 runners

## C/D winners

BRANSTON ABBY 4/93. Much better on good to soft in 1993 and 1994.

MASTER PLANNER 8/93. A difficult judgement was required here.

He had won over course and distance, and last time out (7 May) had won well off 96. For his two and a half-length victory, the Handicapper had increased his mark to 102, 6lb above his highest previous winning mark. Now six years old, there were no special circumstances to suggest that he could beat the Handicapper: he was still in the same stable; he had been a gelding in 1994; and he had not been ridden in a different way. I decided that the new mark would be too much for MASTER PLANNER.

ROGER THE BUTLER same race 1994. After winning this race all out off 94 (Race 918), he had gone on to win again over the course and distance (Race 1529), but this time more comfortably, off a mark of 99. In the rest of the season, he ran seven times without winning, in both Listed races and handicaps. His mark reached a high-point of

106; by the end of the season it was down to 101; and now he was back on his last winning mark of 99.

But in this race he was still 5lb above his winning mark in the same race in 1994, and I decided that his chance could be discounted.

## D winners

AMRON 5/93. A great specialist at Doncaster, he had won his first race in 1994, a Listed race, but had failed to win in handicaps. Held by the Handicapper.

HARD TO FIGURE 8/93 Ayr. Had not won in 1994.

PALACEGATE TOUCH 4/95. Had only won on good or good to soft, and was unsuited by the firm going.

VENTURE CAPITALIST 6/94 Royal Ascot. By winning the Wokingham Handicap, he had shown that he was a high class handicapper. However, he had to be driven right out to win off a mark of 91, and was now 9lb higher. It was difficult to evaluate his 1995 form: winning a 6f Class C stakes in good style at Thirsk (Race 719 22 April) followed by a reasonable run to be fourth in a 7f handicap at Haydock (Race 953 8 May). I could not see him winning this race off a mark of 100.

Although I decided against making a selection in this race, I am sure you will agree that there were some good handicappers in this race with at least chances worth considering in some detail (in particular, MASTER PLANNER, ROGER THE BUTLER, and VENTURE CAPITALIST).

The race result - with VENTURE CAPITALIST first, MASTER PLANNER third, and ROGER THE BUTLER fourth - was nowhere as nearly surprising as the choice of MONAASSIB as favourite. On his only previous race in 1995, he had been soundly beaten by VENTURE CAPITALIST off levels in the Class C stakes at Thirsk (Race 719). They met again on terms 4lb more favourable to MONAASSIB, but the latter had not won a handicap. In fact, he had only won two races: a 6f maiden stakes at Salisbury (Race 837 5 May 1994), albeit beating Lake Coniston; and a four-runner Class C stakes, also over 6f (Race 1994 Haydock 1 July 1994).

With so little chance on the form book, why was MONAASSIB made favourite in such a competitive handicap? The choice was a vote of sympathy for his previous trainer, Alex Scott, who had died in tragic circumstances in 1994, and an expression of faith in his new trainer, Ed Dunlop, son of a famous father (John Dunlop). 'The booking of Walter Swinburn to ride MONAASSIB is significant' was also a thought which occurred to many punters.

17 May YORK (Race 1106 5f Good to firm)

| | | | |
|---|---|---|---|
| 20103-3 | GORINSKY | 7-10-0 | D |
| 00016-0 | PALACEGATE JACK | 4-9-12 | NWH |
| 6002-03 | LORD HIGH ADMIRAL | 7-9-9 | D |
| 1040-21 | BRAVE EDGE | 4-9-7 | D |
| 04200-5 | TUSCAN DAWN | 5-9-5 | D |
| 003-603 | SIR JOEY | 6-9-1 | D |
| 14001-0 | INSIDER TRADER | 4-9-0 | C/D |
| 04034-0 | PRINCESS OBERON | 5-8-13 | D |
| /20000- | ALLWIGHT THEN | 4-8-9 | D |
| 10-1260 | SADDLEHOME | 6-8-6 | C/D |
| 1-12532 | CROFT POOL | 4-8-5 | NWH |
| 00500-0 | MACFARLANE | 7-8-4 | C/D |

| 4000-03 | MAGIC PEARL | 5-8-4 | D |
| 1000-44 | NAME THE TUNE | 4-8-3 | D |
| 436132 | SPENDER | 6-8-2 | D |
| 1323-50 | CROFT IMPERIAL | 8-7-12 | NWH |

16 runners

Before making the analysis, this race seems to be the typical sprint handicap lottery. But a careful check reveals that, although there are three course and distance winners, and ten distance winners, there are only three horses with a worthwhile chance. The result confirmed the analysis in textbook fashion.

## C/D winners

INSIDER TRADER 8/94 won a good class handicap at the August meeting here. He also won his last race of the season, at Catterick, off a mark of 75. Now running off 83, he had shown nothing on his only race to date, but could not be discounted.

MACFARLANE 5/93. Had not won since 1993; and only won on good or good to soft.

SADDLEHOME 10/94. After winning this race off 70, he had won his last race of 1994, at York off 73. Now on 75, he had a strong chance.

## D winners

ALLWIGHT THEN 9/93 Redcar nursery. Not won since 1993.

BRAVE EDGE 4/95 Sandown. Had won his last race well, and could not be discounted.

GORINSKY 9/94 Ascot. Held off this mark (97) at the end of 1994: unlikely to have improved.

LORD HIGH ADMIRAL 5/94 Haydock. Held off this mark (92).

MAGIC PEARL 10/93 Catterick. Only won on good or good to soft.

NAME THE TUNE 8/94 Haydock. Only won on good or good to soft.

PRINCESS OBERON 7/94 Newcastle. Only won on uphill courses.

SIR JOEY 8/94 Ayr. Held by BRAVE EDGE last time out.

SPENDER 4/94 Brighton. Much better on All Weather.

TUSCAN DAWN 8/93 Thirsk. Not won since 1993.

## Selection: SADDLEHOME. Challengers: BRAVE EDGE, INSIDER TRADER.

BRAVE EDGE, a reasonable favourite at 9/2, was held up, came with a good run inside the final furlong and won well by one and a half lengths, from SADDLEHOME. INSIDER TRADER, at 10-1, soon lost touch and was a well beaten fourteenth. The Handicapper was impressed with BRAVE EDGE, and raised his mark by 9lb, enough to stop him winning for the rest of the season.

# How to Beat the Handicapper

20 May THIRSK (Race 1179 7f Good to firm)

| | | | |
|---|---|---|---|
| 0000-05 | CELESTIAL KEY | 5-9-12 | H |
| 1300-04 | KNAVE'S ASH | 4-9-11 | D |
| 0025-00 | SELHURSTPARK FLYER | 4-9-7 | H |
| 062202 | QUEENS CONSUL | 5-9-1 | H |
| 006040- | HI NOD | 5-9-1 | C/D |
| 0-4044 | CELESTIAL CHOIR | 5-8-13 | NWH |
| 00430-3 | JATO | 6-8-12 | C/D |
| 000041 | PERSIAN AFFAIR | 4-8-8 | D |
| 00-0010 | PRIDE OF PENDLE | 6-8-6 | H |
| 640150 | CHINOUR | 7-8-1 | H |
| 10040-2 | SARMATIAN | 4-8-0 | H |
| 2442-03 | CRAIGIE BOY | 5-7-11 | H |
| 100620 | PINE RIDGE LAD | 5-7-7 | H |

13 runners

Although this was a field of experienced handicappers, as only CELESTIAL CHOIR had not won a handicap, 7f is a specialists' distance, and 8 of the runners were at the 'wrong' distance.

## C/D winners

HI NOD same race 1994. After winning here first time out, he had lost his next eight races, bringing his mark down 5lb below his 1994 win.

JATO 4/94. After winning here early in the season, he had won one more race, at Pontefract, when rated 67. Now running off 76, 25lb above his last course and distance win, he was held by the Handicapper.

## D winners

KNAVE'S ASH 5/94 York. Lightly raced, and gelded since 1994, was this a dark horse, being cleverly placed by the canny Michael Stoute?

PERSIAN AFFAIR 5/95 Brighton. A winner last time out, could not be discounted.

Selection: HI NOD.          Challengers: KNAVE'S ASH, PERSIAN AFFAIR.

How wrong can you be! CELESTIAL KEY won quite easily, with HI NOD's effort petering out at the 3 furlong marker, to finish with only three behind him, two of which were KNAVE'S ASH and PERSIAN AFFAIR. JATO was a well beaten second. Later in the season, HI NOD showed his liking for this distance by three wins in much better company, finishing off with a good win at York, running off 17lb higher than in this race.

22 May BATH (Race 1202 1m 5y Good to firm)

| | | | |
|---|---|---|---|
| 04222- | LEGENDARY LEAP | 5-9-12 | NWR |
| 000-00 | PETER ROWLEY | 6-9-7 | NWR |
| 0-00 | SURGIVA | 3-7-11 | NWR |
| 5505/00 | JAIRZINHO | 6-9-7 | NWH |
| 0000/0- | ESTHAL | 5-9-2 | NWH |
| 0046-10 | DOMINION'S DREAM | 3-9-1 | NWR |
| 343140 | MASTER MILLFIELD | 3-9-0 | NWR |

| 5000-35 | VANBOROUGH LAD | 6-8-13 | C/D |
| 10-5432 | WENTBRIDGE LAD | 5-8-13 | NWH |
| 0-0661 | FLEET CADET | 4-8-11 | H |
| 204043- | DUNGEON DANCER | 3-8-10 | NWH |
| 00-0 | BORN TO PLEASE | 3-8-9 | NWR |
| 0000-51 | ALMAPA | 3-8-8 | NWH |
| 100-004 | SHAYNES DOMAIN | 4-8-5 | NWH |
| 50425-3 | RUNIC SYMBOL | 4-8-3 | NWR |
| 0000-00 | NOEPROB | 5-8-3 | NWH |
| 006- | RING THE CHIEF | 3-7-12 | NWR |

17 runners

After a series of competitive or difficult handicaps, this race was something of a freak. The topweight was rated 65, and it looked like an average weak handicap: but not at all. The first check showed that seven runners had not won a handicap, and that eight had not even won a race. A closer look at the form figures showed that 10 of the runners had been tried over the All-Weather, and, by coincidence, had been aimed at a modest handicap at a minor meeting.

### C/D winners

VANBOROUGH LAD same race 1994. He had to be driven right out to win, and lost his next seven races, bringing his mark back down again to 51. Given the style of his victory, I would not have considered him for any other course and distance race, but it was worth taking a chance in the same race. It must be emphasised that a selection on these grounds is independent of the strength of the race.

### D winners

None.

Selection: VANBOROUGH LAD.    Challengers: None.

As I had hoped, WENTBRIDGE LAD was favourite, at 9-2. He had not won on turf since 1992, and was made favourite presumably on the strength of a 'promising' run on the All-Weather last time out. Looking at this race more closely, I noticed that he had stayed on well in the final furlong of a 1m 1f 79y race at Wolverhampton. The plausible argument in his favour was that he would be suited by Bath's stiff uphill final four furlongs.

VANBOROUGH LAD won at 8-1, in exactly the same manner and by exactly the same distance as he had in the same race in 1994: all out, a short head (on this occasion, from WENTBRIDGE LAD).

24 May GOODWOOD (Race 1241 6f Good to firm)

| 402-150 | PALACEGATE TOUCH | 5-10-0 | D |
| 40100-0 | NO EXTRAS | 5-9-12 | D |
| 0065-00 | MY BEST VALENTINE | 5-9-7 | H |
| 001-000 | HOW'S YER FATHER | 9-9-5 | C/D |
| 0-10615 | CASTLEREA LAD | 6-9-4 | C/D |
| 00012-2 | SWEET MAGIC | 4-8-13 | H |
| 124-564 | THAT MAN AGAIN | 3-8-10 | H |
| 01-152 | GOLDEN LADY | 3-8-10 | D |

# How to Beat the Handicapper

152006    INVOCATION                    8-7-13    C/D

9 runners

This was an average handicap - not difficult to make a selection, and a straightforward type of false-priced favourite.

## C/D winners

CASTLEREA LAD same race 1993. In good form this season, he was still on a handy mark. At the beginning of 1994 he was rated 88, but had not won any of his 10 races. Beginning 1995 on a mark of 76, he had found this season's good to firm going much more to his liking. Last time out (Race 949 Doncaster 6f), carrying a 7lb penalty, he was burdened with 10st 3lb, and rated 86; in this race he was on a more reasonable 82, carrying 9st 4lb.

HOW'S YER FATHER 6/93. Held by the Handicapper.

INVOCATION 6/94. Had shown nothing on the turf since winning here in June 1994.

## D winners

GOLDEN LADY 4/95 Brighton. Just failed to win at Chester 5f 16y last time out, and raised 4lb for this defeat! Held by the Handicapper.

NO EXTRAS 4/93 Lingfield. For his last win, in April 1993, by two lengths, he had been raised 17lb. Held by the Handicapper.

PALACEGATE TOUCH 4/95 Ripon. Unsuited by the going, as he was much better on good to soft.

Selection: CASTLEREA LAD.          Challengers: None.

Sometimes it is very clear that the favourite is at a false price, but hard to see why he has attracted the punters' sympathy. This was an easy case.

SWEET MAGIC had won only one handicap, over 5f 6y at Sandown on 14 July 1994. Off a mark of 64, he had to be hard ridden to win by a short head. He had run once more in 1994, at Goodwood (5f) to be beaten a neck. On his only race this season, again at Sandown over 5f 6y, he had been beaten a neck. For this defeat, his rating had been increased 3lb to 77. The 'reasoning' to make him favourite was that he was effective over Sandown's tough 5f, so that he should do well over Goodwood's easier 6f.

In this case, the public's sympathy was with the trainer rather than with the chances of the horse. The late Jack Holt was a much-liked racecourse figure, equally popular with the press, and was adept at training sprint handicappers. Both Mark Winstanley and 'Man on the Spot' praised the trainer and recommended the horse, for the 'reasoning' set out above. In other circumstances, CASTLEREA LAD, with good recent form, a course and distance winner, and ridden by the brilliant Dettori, would have been a hot favourite.

SWEET MAGIC, a consistent favourite at 9-4, was clearly held, in third place. *Raceform's* comment vindicated my judgement: 'Still in with every chance a furlong from home, he was then tapped for toe.

Five furlongs is probably his trip.'

25 May NEWCASTLE (Race 1268 2m 19y Good to firm)

| 00040-6 | HIGHFLYING | 9-9-11 | C/D |
|---------|-----------|--------|-----|
| 0240-02 | GOOD HAND | 9-9-9 | C/D |
| 0663/2- | BEDEVIL | 5-9-9 | NWR |
| 004610 | CUMBRIAN RHAPSODY | 5-9-6 | H |
| 44505-0 | PROVENCE | 8-9-2 | H |
| 054011- | BALZINO | 6-8-6 | H |
| 5400-11 | NOYAN | 5-8-3 | H |
| 000006/ | LEAP IN THE DARK | 6-7-7 | NWH |

8 runners

This was another case of an average handicap, in which the betting is harder to understand than the form.

## C/D winners

GOOD HAND same race 1994. After winning this race easily in 1994, GOOD HAND lost his next ten races, bringing his mark to 73, 3lb lower than his last win. On his previous race, he had shown a glimmer of form in a five-runner race at Redcar over 2m 4y (Race 1084), but if he had not won the same race in 1994, this would not have been good enough. Fortunately, he was still on 73, and worth a chance.

HIGHFLYING 6/93. Had not won since June 1993.

## D winners

None.

## Selection: GOOD HAND. Challengers: None.

NOYAN had won two 1m 5f handicaps this season. The style of his victories (driven out; gamely) did not suggest that he would be suited by a further three furlongs, on a tough course. So why was he favourite at 15-8? *Sporting Life*'s reasoning was, shall we say, inventive. NOYAN was a tough and genuine hurdler; he seemed to stay three miles over the jumps, so that he can be fancied to stay two miles on the Flat.

GOOD HAND, not much fancied at 4-1, won comfortably by just under a length, from HIGHFLYING. This was his only win of the season. At his age he has to have everything just right, and this was the only race in the season when he did.

27 May HAYDOCK (Race 1304 5f Good to soft)

| 002-030 | LORD HIGH ADMIRAL | 7-10-0 | C/D |
|---------|-------------------|--------|-----|
| /24-001 | ANN'S PEARL | 4-9-8 | D |
| 00-4432 | NAME THE TUNE | 4-9-4 | C/D |
| 05000-0 | ANSELLMAN | 5-9-3 | D |
| 514303- | I'M YOUR LADY | 4-9-2 | NWH |
| 436021 | KING RAMBO | 4-9-1 | NWH |
| 0000-06 | BEAU VENTURE | 7-9-0 | C/D |
| 401/355 | RHYTHMIC DANCER | 7-9-0 | D |
| 0500-04 | MACFARLANE | 7-8-13 | D |

| | | | |
|---|---|---|---|
| 323-500 | CROFT IMPERIAL | 8-8-7 | NWH |
| 120000 | LORD SKY | 4-8-7 | NWH |
| 031-142 | CANOVAS HEART | 6-8-3 | D |
| 1000-04 | SEASIDE MINSTREL | 7-8-0 | D |
| 699066 | GONDO | 8-8-0 | C/D |
| 101460 | ONE FOR JEANNIE | 3-7-12 | NWH |
| 455-003 | SERIOUS HURRY | 7-7-7 | NWH |
| 0-24000 | SONDERISE | 6-7-7 | D |

17 runners

Using this system, you have to let any intuition you may feel about the race or a particular horse give way to what the system indicates. This was an open sprint handicap, with no runner having recent form.

## C/D winners

BEAU VENTURE 8/94. Held by LORD HIGH ADMIRAL in the same race 1994.

GONDO 7/93. Had not won since 1993.

LORD HIGH ADMIRAL same race 1994. Eight losing runs had brought his mark down to 86, 1lb below last year's victory. His form this season had been discouraging, but running in the same race and off a similar mark, made him a selection in this system. He had won on any going.

NAME THE TUNE 9/94. Since winning driven out, his mark had been raised 5lb, to 76. It was perhaps unfortunate that for his last run, a well held second at Ripon, he had been raised 4lb. Held by the Handicapper.

## D winners

ANN'S PEARL 5/95 Bath. Unsuited by the going.

ANSELLMAN 4/94 Newmarket. Held by the Handicapper.

CANOVAS HEART 4/95 Warwick. Well held on his last run, he had been raised 1lb. Firmly gripped by the Handicapper.

MACFARLANE 9/94 Doncaster. Held by the Handicapper.

RHYTHMIC DANCER 7/93 Warwick. Not won since 1993.

SEASIDE MINSTREL 9/94 Pontefract. Held by the Handicapper.

SONDERISE 5/93 Thirsk. Not won since 1993.

## Selection: LORD HIGH ADMIRAL.   Challengers: None.

NAME THE TUNE was made 13-2 favourite on the strength of supposedly running well in his previous race, at Ripon. Given the 'negative' form of all the others, then this was a favourite on the 'least worst' principle. Although he had no recent form, 10-1 was a fair price against LORD HIGH ADMIRAL.

This may have been a case of the 'luck of the draw', according to Raceform:

# How to Beat the Handicapper

'Taking advantage of the high draw, LORD HIGH ADMIRAL made all up the stands' rail and had the prize sewn up from some way out.'

29 May DONCASTER (Race 1344 29 May 1m Good)

| | | | |
|---|---|---|---|
| 161310- | PARLIAMENT PIECE | 9-9-10 | H |
| 150-003 | MIDNIGHT JAZZ | 5-9-9 | C/D |
| 6003-00 | KHAYRAPOUR | 5-9-5 | NWH |
| 110622 | JUST HARRY | 4-9-1 | D |
| 5441-16 | BETTERGETON | 3-9-0 | D |
| -114-00 | HALMANERROR | 5-8-12 | H |
| 000006- | OOH AH CANTONA | 4-8-11 | NWH |
| 065040- | PETONELLAJILL | 5-8-8 | NWH |
| 040-4 | GYPSY LOVE | 3-8-7 | NWR |
| 5400-00 | MOVE SMARTLY | 5-8-4 | D |
| 00-0040 | AWESOME VENTURE | 5-8-2 | NWH |
| 000/00- | BUSTER | 7-7-12 | H |
| 000-64 | POYLE JEZEBELLE | 4-7-12 | NWR |
| 0-03614 | SWEET MATE | 3-7-7 | H |

14 runners

A much weaker race, with almost half the runners not having won a handicap or a race, but with not just one, but two straightforward false-priced favourites.

## C/D winners

MIDNIGHT JAZZ same race 1994. Had shown no form this season, but now running off a mark 3lb below that of his 1994 victory.

## D winners

BETTERGETON 4/95 Ripon. After winning quite well at Ripon, in his only other race this season, he had been put back to 7f 122y at Chester. Not unduly punished by the Handicapper, he could not be discounted.

Selection: MIDNIGHT JAZZ.          Challengers: BETTERGETON.

JUST HARRY 10/94 Nottingham. Runs well on All Weather, but his last turf win was off 47, 17lb below his current mark. Held by the Handicapper.

MOVE SMARTLY 6/94 Nottingham. Now on the same mark as that of his solitary handicap victory. Nothing in his subsequent form suggested that he could make it two wins.

GYPSY LOVE was nearest at the finish last time out (Race 1172 20 May Newbury 7f 64y), but still had not won a race of any description. Presumably it was the magic names of P W Chapple-Hyam and R E Sangster which accounted for her being 7-2 joint favourite, along the lines of: 'She would not have been sent all the way to Doncaster unless she had a chance.'

Perhaps the equally magic name of Pat Eddery caused punters to overlook the fact that joint favourite KHAYRAPOUR had not won a handicap. Was the reasoning on the lines of 'The booking of Pat Eddery is significant'?

# How to Beat the Handicapper

Same race winners in this category tend to be all or nothing, first or last. MIDNIGHT JAZZ was a definite zero, as he looked misleadingly well but was tailed off last, beaten twenty lengths.

This is where you must look optimistically to the future. BETTERGETON quickened to lead over one furlong out, and was ridden out to win by a long-looking length. Later in the season (Race 2117), at the same course and distance, he won in pretty much the same style.

31 May RIPON (Race 1414 6f Good to firm)

| | | | |
|---|---|---|---|
| 0-043 | LOUGH ERNE | 3-9-7 | NWR |
| 05-0 | FIRE BLAST | 3-9-6 | NWR |
| 160-10 | THE SCYTHIAN | 3-9-1 | C/D |
| 01560-3 | TEDBURROW | 3-8-13 | NWH |
| 60-221 | SHOWERY | 3-8-13 | D |
| 342033 | RUSSIAN HEROINE | 3-8-9 | H |
| 551305 | SPECIAL-K | 3-8-8 | NWH |
| 032-421 | HI ROCK | 3-8-8 | NWH |
| 15512-0 | FAIRY FAY | 3-8-6 | NWH |
| 63-0550 | PERFECT BERTIE | 3-8-5 | NWR |
| 0060-00 | BLUSHING GRENADIER | 3-8-2 | NWR |
| 6040-66 | GARLANDE D'OR | 3-8-1 | NWR |
| 3000-04 | WESTCOURT PRINCESS | 3-8-1 | NWR |
| 60-062- | LE BAL | 3-7-11 | NWR |
| 000-5 | CAROL AGAIN | 3-7-8 | NWR |

15 runners

This was another freak race like that of VANBOROUGH LAD (see above (Race 1202, 22 May), since out of the 15 runners, eight had not won a race, and four had not won a handicap. However, this time the selection was much more clear cut.

## C/D winners

THE SCYTHIAN 4/95. In his only subsequent race, at Chester (Race 999 10 May) he had been well beaten. Because of the oddities of that course, I discounted that run.

## D winners

SHOWERY 5/95 Haydock apprentice. Form taken from apprentice races is usually misleading: exclude.

## Selection: THE SCYTHIAN.    Challengers: None.

In such a weak race, you could say that SHOWERY had something of a chance, even though she had only won an apprentice race. But why should she be a 6-5 favourite? A set of plausible reasons supported her case: she had won easily; she was on the same handicap mark; and her apprentice could claim 5lb against senior jockeys.

Yet in addition to mistrusting the form of an apprentice handicap, there were two other factors weighing against SHOWERY: her win was over a different type of course (an uphill finish); and on good going. By contrast, THE SCYTHIAN had won a 'proper' handicap over course, distance and going, and at 10-1 was good value.

THE SCYTHIAN won fairly easily, with SHOWERY finding this too competitive and finishing a well-held third.

2 June BATH (Race 1444 2m 1f 34y Good)

| 300-030 | BARDOLPH | 8-10-0 | D |
|---------|----------|--------|---|
| 126-000 | PARADISE NAVY | 6-9-10 | H |
| 535535 | TURRET | 4-8-9 | NWH |
| 11-1100 | ART FORM | 8-9-8 | D |
| 456-550 | LADY VALENSINA | 4-9-3 | NWR |
| 045-210 | INCHCAILLOCH | 6-8-12 | C/D |
| 3466/03 | TAMARPOUR | 8-8-12 | D |
| 50465-0 | ALLMOSA | 6-8-11 | H |
| 56056/2 | FRENCH IVY | 8-8-9 | D |
| 53215-0 | SARAZAR | 6-8-1 | C/D |
| 0/30/0 | SURCOAT | 8-7-7 | H |
| 02/3-0 | ACCESS SUN | 8-7-7 | NWH |
| 215653 | WHO'S THE BEST | 5-7-7 | H |
| 0000-00 | LAJADHAL | 6-7-7 | NWR |

14 runners

This was a reassuringly straightforward handicap, with a readily identifiable false-priced favourite.

## C/D winners

INCHCAILLOCH 5/95. After winning quite well here, his only other race (Race 1189 21 May) before returning to course, distance and going, was at Newbury, quite a different type of course. This run should be discounted.

SARAZAR 7/94. Well beaten by INCHCAILLOCH, last time out, over course and distance.

## D winners

ART FORM 5/92 Goodwood. Runs well on All Weather, but not won on turf since May 1992.

BARDOLPH 11/93 Doncaster. No form in 1994; still 2lb above winning mark in November 1993.

FRENCH IVY 8/91 Chester. Despite being well held by INCHCAILLOCH, was 1lb worse off for their last race (May 1995).

TAMARPOUR 6/91 Newcastle. Not won since 1991.

Selection: INCHCAILLOCH.    Challengers: None.

TAMARPOUR had a wonderful story. In 1991, he had won a high class handicap, the Northumberland Plate; in the previous two seasons, he had been off the course; and he was trained by Martin Pipe. The only problem was that he had no form - he had only won one handicap, four years ago. Last time out, he had run on well in a 1m 7f race (Race 1328 Warwick 27 May), but this was two furlongs further. Against

# How to Beat the Handicapper

INCHCAILLOCH's more prosaic virtues, he certainly attracted the sympathy vote to be 4-1 joint favourite.

Paul Eddery rode a very good race on INCHCAILLOCH (the 4-1 joint favourite), bringing him with a good run inside the final furlong, to beat FRENCH IVY, with TAMARPOUR a well beaten fourth. One can only hope that INCHCAILLOCH will be like that other Bath stalwart, also trained by Jeff King, CHUCKLESTONE.

5 June WINDSOR (Race 1513 1m 3f 135y Good)

| 36-0204 | SAGASAN | 4-10-0 | NWR |
|---------|---------|--------|-----|
| 0013-6 | QUIVIRA | 4-9-12 | C/D |
| 00/01- | BIRD ISLAND | 4-9-12 | NWH |
| 031S00/ | PULMICORT | 5-9-11 | H |
| 0400/03 | PLATINI | 4-9-11 | NWR |
| 043-0 | SAAFI | 4-9-10 | NWR |
| 035100- | SUPREME STAR | 4-9-7 | NWH |
| 00024 | BOLD MICK | 4-9-5 | H |
| 041600- | CASUAL WATER | 4-9-4 | D |
| 30600-3 | SCENIC DANCER | 7-9-4 | C/D |
| 0/0000- | VLADIVOSTOK | 5-9-3 | NWR |
| 00-03 | WIZZY LIZZY | 4-9-2 | NWR |
| 200-0 | SAFE SECRET | 4-9-2 | NWR |
| 00420-0 | SINCLAIR LAD | 7-9-1 | H |
| 30030-0 | BEE BEAT | 7-8-13 | NWH |
| 30-0034 | HI-AUD | 3-8-12 | H |
| 50/00-0 | FORMIDABLE LASS | 4-8-10 | NWR |
| 00-00 | BORN TO PLEASE | 3-8-10 | NWR |
| 0300-60 | CAPTAIN STARLIGHT | 4-8-9 | NWH |
| 00/400- | CHEVELEY DANCER | 7-8-8 | NWR |

20 runners

Another fairly straightforward race, with the discouraging title of the 'Onandonandon Handicap'! - certainly it must have expressed the feelings of the trainers who did not see any change in the fortunes of the nine ever hopeful maidens, and the four runners which had not won a handicap.

## C/D winners

QUIVIRA 6/94. Had to struggle to win off 51, now on 56: held by the Handicapper.

SCENIC DANCER same race 1994. Ran quite well last time (Race 1166 20 May) over a shorter distance, and was now on the same mark (48) as last year.

## D winners

CASUAL WATER 6/94 Catterick. Held by the Handicapper.

Selection: SCENIC DANCER.     Challengers: None.

The two course and distance winners were in the first three - but in the 'wrong' order, and both outpointed by HI-AUD. Although SCENIC DANCER, the 7-2 favourite, was slowly away, and took a long time to get into gear, there were no excuses for defeat. HI-AUD led well over one furlong out, and ran on to win by a comfortable four lengths.

# How to Beat the Handicapper

7 June WARWICK (Race 1543 1m 2f 169y Good)

| | | | |
|---|---|---|---|
| 13/5-00 | LOMAS | 4-10-0 | NWH |
| 162025- | LUCAYAN CAY | 4-9-13 | NWH |
| 14540-6 | MUSEUM | 4-9-11 | NWH |
| 230-600 | SHANGHAI VENTURE | 4-9-9 | NWH |
| 3520-06 | SCOTTISH BAMBI | 7-9-0 | C/D |
| 600412 | HAROLDON | 6-9-0 | C/D |
| 46040- | PEACHES POLLY | 5-8-10 | NWR |
| 000-030 | PINK BRIEF | 4-8-8 | NWH |
| 141012 | LARN FORT | 5-8-4 | D |
| 60-051 | MYFONTAINE | 8-8-3 | C/D |

10 runners

There was a very obvious selection in this weak race, but at the same time I had marked another runner down as a likely false-priced favourite.

## C/D winners

HAROLDON 5/95 held by MYFONTAINE over course and distance last time out.

MYFONTAINE 5/95. Had won 5 times over the course and distance, and won his previous race 'with a fair bit in hand' (*Raceform* Race 1324 27 May).

SCOTTISH BAMBI 5/92. Readers with a good memory will recall that he was a useful handicapper in 1993. Unfortunately, in 1994 he seemed to have lost his way, and his two runs this season offered no encouragement.

## D winners

LARN FORT 5/95. Held last time out on 54, he had been raised 2lb for a hard-fought second place. The Handicapper was unrelenting.

Selection: MYFONTAINE. Challengers: None.

My hopes that MUSEUM, second favourite in the *Sporting Life* betting show, might be favourite, were disappointed, as MYFONTAINE was always clear, at 9-4. For once I disagreed with *Raceform*, which reported that he had won 'driven out', whereas it seemed to me that he had won with something in hand. HAROLDON got a bit closer to MYFONTAINE this time, but the latter was never in danger.

12 June WARWICK (Race 1658 10m 2f 169y Good to firm)

| | | | |
|---|---|---|---|
| 0-00511 | MYFONTAINE | 8-10-1 | C/D |
| 56-5500 | LADY VALENSINA | 4-9-9 | NWR |
| 20-0 | DANCING DESTINY | 3-9-7 | NWR |
| 00-4 | BELL CONTRACTORS | 3-9-5 | NWR |
| 000-240 | PORTE BELLOCH | 4-8-10 | NWH |
| 10-1002 | ROLLING WATERS | 5-8-7 | NWR |
| -000 | SHEPHERDS REST | 3-8-7 | NWR |
| 6-35400 | LEXUS | 7-8-5 | D |

8 runners

From this point in the season, the selection process is much simpler, for two reasons: winners of the same race have to have won in the current season; and non-winners this season are to be considered false-priced favourites.

Here I was tempted to break one of my rules, so the race is included for the purposes of illustration only.

## C/D winners

MYFONTAINE 6/95. I relied on my own reading of the previous race here, and did not agree with *Raceform*'s comment that MYFONTAINE had been 'driven out.' However, he now carried 10st 1lb, and I have made it a fixed rule never to bet on horses carrying more than 10st. Although he seemed an outstanding chance, rules are rules in this system, and he had to be passed over.

## D winners

LEXUS 6/93 Yarmouth apprentice. Not won since 1993.

## Selection: None.

For the sake of 1lb, it seemed rather pedantic to rule out MYFONTAINE. Yet the long-term record shows that 10st is the barrier which few horses can leap over, so MYFONTAINE had to be passed over.

If it had been a selection, would it have been ludicrous to expect that there would be a false-priced favourite? It turned out to be not a hypothetical question, as DANCING DESTINY was the 15-8 market leader. On her only race this season (Race 1128 Salisbury 18 May) she had been beaten just over eight lengths in a 1m 1f 209y maiden stakes. Perhaps she had been hampered? running on strongly at the finish? Not according to *Raceform*, which stated that she had been 'never near to challenge.' Her trainer, J R Fanshawe, is a very clever trainer of fillies, but this was a case of highly exaggerated expectations.

MYFONTAINE won this easily enough, to record his seventh course and distance win. Headed well over one furlong out, DANCING DESTINY could not quicken, and although only beaten one length, really had no chance with the winner.

14 June BEVERLEY (Race 1679 7f 100y Good to firm)

| | | | |
|---|---|---|---|
| 050100- | CAVATINA | 5-10-0 | H |
| 220-033 | SUPEROO | 9-9-13 | D |
| 300-602 | OCHOS RIOS | 4-9-8 | D |
| 0-00500 | BALLARD RING | 4-9-3 | H |
| 0000-05 | PALLIUM | 7-9-1 | H |
| 00-0001 | LANCASHIRE LIFE | 4-9-10 | H |
| 0210-00 | STAR OF GOLD | 3-8-13 | NWH |
| 3-61600 | TWIN CREEKS | 4-8-12 | NWR |
| 0-50461 | IT'S ACADEMIC | 3-8-10 | NWH |
| 6-04264 | MURPHY'S GOLD | 4-8-9 | D |
| 004032 | KILNAMARTYRA GIRL | 5-8-4 | D |
| 640-000 | STATOMIST | 3-8-2 | NWR |
| 3-06131 | EURO SCEPTIC | 3-8-1 | C/D |
| 040-660 | GARLANDE D'OR | 3-7-12 | NWR |
| 361466 | SWEET MATE | 3-7-11 | NWR |
| 100000- | HENRY WILL | 11-7-7 | C/D |

# How to Beat the Handicapper

16 runners

This was a case where the *Raceform/Raceform Update* reports would arrive too late for the weekly subscriber. There are only three or four occasions per season affecting the kind of races which this system applies to, but in any case you can get round the problem either by watching races yourself, or subscribing to the mid-weekly edition of *Raceform*.

As Beverley is one of my star courses, I had watched the 7f 100y handicap on the previous Wednesday, won by EURO SCEPTIC. As it happened, the *Raceform* observers came to the same conclusion ('ridden and ran on') and commented that he 'really likes this awkward track.'

## C/D winners

EURO SCEPTIC 6/95. Won last time out.

HENRY WILL 6/94. No form since last win; held by the Handicapper.

## D winners

* I take 7f at other courses to be equivalent to the 7f 100y distance of this race - not entirely satisfactory, but nearer to the mark than 1m.

KILNAMARTYRA GIRL 7/94 Newcastle. Second last time out, but raised 2lb. Held off this mark; not won this season.

MURPHY'S GOLD 6/94 Carlisle. Last win over 1m, so put back in distance; not won this season.

OCHOS RIOS 9/94 Haydock. Held by EURO SCEPTIC last time out.

SUPEROO 5/94 Catterick. Unable to quicken last time out, but raised 2lb. Not won this season.

Selection: EURO SCEPTIC.        Challengers: None.

There was a very good story here. IT'S ACADEMIC had won a maiden apprentice stakes last time out, over 7f at Catterick. Even though she had been unpenalised for a rather modest success, there was not much to get excited about until you looked for the names of the jockey and trainer. The apprentice had been replaced by Kieren Fallon, and, as before, the trainer was Lynda Ramsden. Who in their right journalistic mind could not congratulate himself on seeing through such a transparent plot?

IT'S ACADEMIC was a sound false-priced favourite at 9-2, and ran as well as her form suggested, a well-beaten fifth. Unfortunately, EURO SCEPTIC did as well as the parliamentary rebels of the same name, and at about the same time. He struggled well...into third place, behind MURPHY'S GOLD and KILNAMARTYRA GIRL.

16 June SANDOWN (Race 1753 1m 2f 7y Good to firm)

| | | | |
|---|---|---|---|
| 3221-06 | GREEN CRUSADER | 4-9-12 | D |
| 4411-10 | SPECIAL DAWN | 5-9-2 | C/D |
| 2/210-0 | AEROKING | 4-9-2 | NWH |
| 3125-60 | MENTOR | 3-8-9 | NWH |

| 22-1 | RAHY ZOMAN | 3-8-5 | NWH |
|---|---|---|---|
| 410-425 | MIHRIZ | 3-8-3 | NWH |

6 runners

Even 0-100 handicaps, with a top weight officially rated 92, at a high class course like Sandown, sometimes attract very weak fields; and even then, you can find a false-priced favourite.

## C/D winners

SPECIAL DAWN 5/94. After winning at Kempton, he had been beaten at Newmarket, and seemed to need a turning track.

## D winners

GREEN CRUSADER 9/94 Newbury. Only won on good to soft or soft. Unsuited by the going.

Selection: SPECIAL DAWN.       Challengers: None.

Perhaps the lightly-raced course and distance winner, SPECIAL DAWN, trained by a master (John Dunlop) was too 'obvious'. But there was nothing very obvious about the chances of the 2-1 favourite, RAHY ZOMAN, winner of a 1m 1f maiden at Goodwood.

SPECIAL DAWN won with such authority, that he almost made 9-4 seem a generous price.

16 June YORK (Race 1765 5f Good to firm)

| 31206-2 | SAINT EXPRESS | 5-10-0 | C/D |
|---|---|---|---|
| 424-010 | ASHTINA | 10-9-13 | D |
| 3-00606 | CALL ME I'M BLUE | 5-9-11 | D |
| 11U2-00 | SEA-DEER | 6-9-10 | D |
| 1142-00 | CROFTERS CEILIDH | 3-9-9 | C/D |
| 00-0010 | BENZOE | 5-8-11 | H |
| 000-030 | MAGIC PEARL | 5-8-11 | H |
| 443224 | NAME THE TUNE | 4-8-10 | D |
| 2000-02 | ALLWIGHT THEN | 4-8-7 | D |
| 225-100 | HICKORY BLUE | 5-8-5 | D |
| 34015 | ELLE SHAPED | 5-8-4 | D |
| 066450 | TENOR | 4-7-12 | D |
| 40-3112 | LADY SHERIFF | 4-7-7 | D |

13 runners

This race is included to illustrate a number of points, and to show how strong the temptation can be to over-rule a methodical approach. In this case, it would have been to your advantage; in the long run, it is not.

## C/D winners

CROFTERS CEILIDH 7/94. After winning a nursery, he had been running in Listed races. Too high in the handicap.

# How to Beat the Handicapper

SAINT EXPRESS same race 1994. Following the rules, SAINT EXPRESS should have been excluded automatically. Although he had won this race well in 1994 (Race 1528), he was now 10lb higher in the handicap (rated 94). But seeing that he had been second in his only run this season, and that he was trained by the very capable Mary Reveley, I was tempted to delve into his past.

I found that in 1994 he had been with three trainers: Mick Channon, Nigel Tinkler, and Mary Reveley, for whom his first race had been on 17 September. Last time out, on good to soft going which did not suit him, *Raceform* had commented: '...appears better on top of the ground, put in a sterling effort and will not be long in winning.'

Despite being beaten three-parts of a length, SAINT EXPRESS was raised 4lb for this promising run. If he had been left on the same mark, it would have been a much more difficult decision, but he now seemed to have too much to do.

## D winners

ALLWIGHT THEN 8/93 Redcar. Not won since 1993.

ASHTINA 5/95 Chester. Held by the Handicapper.

CALL ME I'M BLUE 9/93 Ascot. Not won since September 1993.

ELLE SHAPED 6/95 Chester. Won twice at Chester. May be more suited by Chester, but can not be discounted.

HICKORY BLUE 5/95 Lingfield. Held by LADY SHERIFF.

LADY SHERIFF 6/95 Thirsk. May be held by the Handicapper, since she was raised 1lb for a good run last time out, a neck second at Goodwood. However, she is in good form, and can not be discounted.

MAGIC PEARL 10/93 Catterick. Only won on good or good to soft.

NAME THE TUNE 9/94 Haydock. Not won this season.

SEA-DEER 7/94 Goodwood. Held by the Handicapper.

TENOR 4/95 Thirsk. Held by LADY SHERIFF.

Selection: None.

It was a pity that there was no selection, as there was a clear false-priced 11-2 favourite, SEA-DEER. Trained by the popular Jack Holt, he had not won this season in two outings over 6f (Races 1174, 1316). Press comment was along the lines: put back to his best distance, SEA-DEER is on a handy mark. The latter point was quite unfounded, as his most recent victory (Race 2584 Goodwood 27 July 1994) had been by a length and a quarter, off a mark of 79. He was now 11lb higher, and had not won this season.

SAINT EXPRESS led one furlong out and held on well to win by half a length, with SEA-DEER a never-dangerous fifth.

17 June SANDOWN (Race 1794 1m 6f Good to firm)

004133-  TUKANO                        4-9-13      NWH

67

| /5/014- | IVOR'S FLUTTER | 6-9-12 | H |
|---|---|---|---|
| 5030-06 | PEMBRIDGE PLACE | 4-9-10 | NWH |
| 433101 | JOHNS ACT | 5-9-9 | H |
| 11-3335 | CUANGO | 4-9-7 | H |
| 5-211 | EMBRACING | 3-8-10 | C/D |
| 05-0 | FAST FORWARD | 4-8-8 | NWR |
| 0-00312 | REQUESTED | 8-8-6 | D |
| 0013-24 | ELA MAN HOWA | 4-8-3 | NWH |
| 011253 | JARAAB | 4-7-8 | NWR |
| 0/3403- | RUN HIGH | 12-7-7 | C/D |

11 runners

This was only a slightly more competitive race than the one run on the previous day at the same course (see above, Race 1753). A hoped-for false-priced favourite did not materialise, but, to repeat the point, the race was no different from others in which a false price *was* available about the favourite.

## C/D winners

EMBRACING 5/95 Won last time out.

RUN HIGH 5/90. Not won since a race September 1990.

## D winners

REQUESTED 5/95 Newmarket. Held by EMBRACING last time out.

## Selection: EMBRACING.   Challengers: None.

I hoped that REQUESTED might be fancied to reverse the form with EMBRACING, but the latter was always a firm favourite at 15-8. She confirmed the form of the previous race almost to the pound, winning well enough to make you think 'Well perhaps I should consider backing such stand out bets even at a short price.' Think again and don't be tempted!

For each-way backers, REQUESTED seemed to be fair value at 7-1, certainly much better than the 6-1 second favourite, PEMBRIDGE PLACE.

20 June THIRSK (Race 1844 1m 4f Good to firm)

| 0-00451 | LOOKINGFORARAINBOW | 7-9-13 | C/D |
|---|---|---|---|
| /1031-6 | KINGS CAY | 4-9-7 | D |
| 505115- | FIRST BID | 8-9-2 | D |
| 54-2414 | MR TOWSER | 4-8-11 | NWR |
| 122051 | STEVIE'S WONDER | 5-8-8 | D |
| 53-0552 | NORTH ARDAR | 5-8-0 | H |
| 30310-6 | PERSIAN SOLDIER | 8-7-7 | C/D |

7 runners
A bread-and-butter handicap, with the selection losing for an unusual reason.

## C/D winners

LOOKINGFORARAINBOW 6/95. Won last time out.

# How to Beat the Handicapper

PERSIAN SOLDIER 7/94. Well beaten by LOOKINGFORARAINBOW last time out.

## D winners

FIRST BID 9/94 Beverley. Last two wins over longer distances.

KINGS CAY 7/94 Salisbury. Not won this season.

STEVIE'S WONDER 6/95 Leicester. Trained by Mick Ryan, a dark horse.

Selection: LOOKINGFORARAINBOW. Challengers: STEVIE'S WONDER.

It was difficult to see what could be made favourite other than LOOKINGFORARAINBOW, and he was always solid at 5-2. In the race, he collided with the rails when leaving the back straight. It was too late to recover, and he finished third. Accounting for this result conservatively, I decided to write it down as a defeat.

NORTH ARDAR, a good handicapper but not, so I thought, at this distance, ran on to lead close home.

30 June NEWCASTLE (Race 2060 5f Firm)

| | | | |
|---|---|---|---|
| 31041-4 | TAKADOU | 4-9-10 | H |
| 340-014 | PRINCESS OBERON | 5-9-9 | C/D |
| 200-500 | TUSCAN DAWN | 5-9-6 | D |
| 0-00102 | BENZOE | 5-9-5 | H |
| 0012-23 | SWEET MAGIC | 4-9-1 | D |
| 432244 | NAME THE TUNE | 4-8-12 | D |
| 401535 | ELLE SHAPED | 5-8-9 | D |
| 000-020 | ALLWIGHT THEN | 4-8-9 | D |
| 5-11052 | WHITE SORRELL | 4-8-5 | NWR |
| 506311 | SHADOW JURY | 5-8-1 | D |
| 144-000 | HIGH RANKING | 3-8-0 | D |
| 213101 | RICH GLOW | 4-7-11 | D |

12 runners

The Gosforth Park Cup is a competitive race, which requires more than a course and distance win for a selection. Nine of the twelve runners had won over the distance, and one appeared to have top-class form.

## C/D winners

PRINCESS OBERON 7/94. In good form this season, had won well at Newmarket, and then been unplaced over 6f at York. Back to course and distance, she appeared to have every chance.

## D winners

ALLWIGHT THEN 9/93 Redcar. Not won since 9/93.

ELLE SHAPED 6/95 Chester. Unsuited by the course.

HIGH RANKING 8/94 Haydock. Not won this season.

# How to Beat the Handicapper

NAME THE TUNE 9/94 Haydock. Held by PRINCESS OBERON at Newmarket.

RICH GLOW 6/95 Ayr. Only won at Ayr - unsuited by the course.

SHADOW JURY 6/95 Hamilton. Hard ridden to win - outclassed here.

SWEET MAGIC 7/94 Sandown. Not won this season.

TAKADOU 9/94 Newmarket. Not won this season.

Selection: PRINCESS OBERON.    Challengers: None.

SWEET MAGIC was once again a false-priced favourite, for different reasons (see Race 1241). This time, he was back to his distance - but in no way did this alter the fact that he had yet to win this season. Under any circumstances, 5-2 is a short price in a sprint handicap.

It was not much consolation to see SWEET MAGIC in second place when PRINCESS OBERON could manage no better than sixth. NAME THE TUNE, driven out for a hard-fought success, was rather a surprising winner.

2 July DONCASTER (Race 2117 1m Firm)

| | | | |
|---|---|---|---|
| 0-06020 | MELLOTTIE | 10-10-0 | C/D |
| 30-0000 | NEW CAPRICORN | 5-9-12 | H |
| 160-050 | FOREVER DIAMONDS | 8-9-10 | D |
| 000000 | MASTER BEVELED | 5-9-6 | D |
| 20-1003 | WESTERN GENERAL | 4-9-5 | D |
| 32-0511 | UP IN FLAMES | 4-9-3 | D |
| 41-1611 | BETTERGETON | 3-9-2 | C/D |
| 0-00044 | PROMISE FULFILLED | 4-9-0 | NWH |
| 3-01024 | SANDMOOR CHAMBRAY | 4-8-13 | H |
| 000255 | FAME AGAIN | 3-8-4 | D |
| 000205 | KEMO SABO | 3-8-3 | NWH |

11 runners

After a trying month ('flaming June' in every sense), it was a relief to begin July with a success: a boringly obvious selection, opposed by two seductive favourites.

## C/D winners

BETTERGETON 5/95. Since winning here, won a five-runner race at Ripon, over the distance.

MELLOTTIE 9/92 Not won since 10/93.

## D winners

FAME AGAIN 9/94 Pontefract. Not won on the going; not won this season.

FOREVER DIAMONDS 5/94 Haydock. Not won this season.

MASTER BEVELED 10/94 Newmarket. Not won this season.

UP IN FLAMES 5/95 Haydock. Won over 1m 114y at Epsom: put back in distance.

WESTERN GENERAL 4/95 Pontefract.

Selection: BETTERGETON.          Challengers: None.

FAME AGAIN had finished fast over 7f at Doncaster, but still had not won this season. Three-year-olds which have not won in their second season can be very expensive, but the Fallon-Ramsden combination persuaded punters to overlook this well known fact. UP IN FLAMES had more to be said for him, but he seemed to need longer distances than one mile. With these two joint favourites at 4-1, BETTERGETON was pushed out to 5-1, fair value for an obvious selection, and won as reassuringly as one could hope for.

6 July CATTERICK (Race 2188 7f Good to firm)

| | | | |
|---|---|---|---|
| 0-01 | KAFANI AL WIDD | 3-9-7 | NWH |
| 534-6 | MOUNTGATE | 3-9-4 | NWH |
| 512044 | MAC'S TAXI | 3-9-0 | C/D |
| 010111 | RUSSIAN HEROINE | 3-8-13 | D |
| 443-6 | AMAZING | 3-8-8 | NWR |
| 400-220 | TAKESHI | 3-8-7 | NWR |
| 312233 | CONCER UN | 3-8-7 | NWH |
| 10-004 | FLAMBORO | 3-8-1 | D |

8 runners

Sometimes your forebodings are confirmed, but you have to learn always to ignore them, if you want to operate systematically.

## C/D winners

MAC'S TAXI 4/95 made all to win here by eight lengths, at the end of April, and had run in a variety of unsuitable races since.

## D winners

FLAMBORO 11/94 Newcastle. Not won this season.

RUSSIAN HEROINE 6/95 Chester. Also won at Edinburgh, and in good form: can not be discounted.

Selection: MAC'S TAXI.    Challengers: RUSSIAN HEROINE.

I wondered whether Michael Stoute's KAFANI AL WIDD might be made favourite on the strength of a reasonably convincing win in a Thirsk maiden, but RUSSIAN HEROINE was always in demand at 9-4. MAC'S TAXI tried to repeat his winning tactics of leading all the way, but he was headed two furlongs out, and that was that. RUSSIAN HEROINE led two furlongs out, and was never seriously challenged.

7 July BEVERLEY (Race 2222 1m 100y Good to firm)

| | | | |
|---|---|---|---|
| 200013 | QUEENS CONSUL | 5-9-10 | C/D |
| 243/0/0 | GYMCRAK TIGER | 5-9-7 | NWH |

# How to Beat the Handicapper

| | | | |
|---|---|---|---|
| 001064 | KINGCHIP BOY | 6-9-6 | D |
| 044030 | CELESTIAL CHOIR | 5-9-6 | D |
| 223222 | JUST HARRY | 4-9-1 | D |
| 361345 | EQUERRY | 4-8-13 | C/D |
| 03301 | SUPEROO | 9-8-13 | H |
| 00-213 | COUREUR | 6-8-12 | C/D |
| 222002 | MONTONE | 5-8-2 | H |
| 426413 | MURPHY'S GOLD | 4-7-11 | D |

10 runners

Competitive handicaps can be found anywhere, and this one was quite a puzzle, with seven out of the ten runners having won over the distance.

### C/D winners

COUREUR 6/95. His win here was followed by one race which could be discounted, as it was over 1m 2f at Redcar, a longer distance and an unsuitable course.

EQUERRY 5/95 Won driven along. Held by COUREUR at Newcastle.

QUEENS CONSUL 7/94 Had won a fillies and mares race at Thirsk in June 1995, but had previously beaten colts and geldings. However, she seemed well held last time at Warwick, and should be discounted.

### D winners

* I take 1m at other courses to be equivalent to the 1m 100y distance of this race

CELESTIAL CHOIR 9/94 Haydock. Not won this season.

JUST HARRY 10/94 Nottingham. Not won this season.

KINGCHIP BOY 5/95 Goodwood. Held by the Handicapper.

MURPHY'S GOLD 7/94 Ayr. Won here over 7f 100y earlier this season. Held by the Handicapper over 1m.

### Selection: COUREUR.    Challengers: None.

COUREUR opened 9-2, and shortened to 3-1, but no other runner was available at a shorter price. The course and distance winners took three of the first four places, but not the vital one, occupied by MURPHY'S GOLD. Was COUREUR as unlucky as *Raceform* suggested: '...badly hampered when KINGCHIP BOY went across him turning out of the back straight....was staying on at the finish.'? As he was only beaten by a neck and a length, perhaps he was, but bookmakers do not pay out on 'should have'.

17 July WINDSOR (Race 2490 1m 2f 7y Good to firm)

| | | | |
|---|---|---|---|
| 1100-05 | PERSIAN ELITE | 4-10-0 | C/D |
| 412261 | HAROLDON | 6-10-0 | D |
| 066- | DOUBLE JEOPARDY | 4-9-12 | NWR |
| 00-0104 | TRADE WIND | 4-9-9 | NWH |

# How to Beat the Handicapper

| 235260 | DUELLO | 4-9-0 | NWR |
| 0223-56 | CONSPICUOUS | 5-8-11 | NWR |
| 0-00051 | DR EDGAR | 3-8-9 | C/D |
| 0440-0 | GRAND APPLAUSE | 5-8-7 | NWR |
| 0-00551 | JUST FLAMENCO | 4-8-4 | C/D |
| 20/4023 | MARCHMAN | 10-8-1 | D |
| 050141 | MIGHTY KINGDOM | 4-7-11 | H |

11 runners

There are two or three races every season, in which it is simply not possible to decide between two or more course and distance winners. As there are so few, it is not worth agonising: they can be easily identified and ignored. For the record, the following example is given.

## C/D winners

DR EDGAR 6/95 last time out.

JUST FLAMENCO 7/95 last time out.

PERSIAN ELITE 8/94 apprentice. Not won this season.

## D winners

HAROLDON 5/95 Warwick. Won previous race over 1m 4f: put back in distance.

MARCHMAN 6/93 Chepstow.

## Selection: None.

Both DR EDGAR and JUST FLAMENCO won easily last time out, in different styles, and I could not decide between them. The race was surprising: neither JUST FLAMENCO (sixth) nor DR EDGAR (last but one) made much of a show. Although they won a race each later in the season, neither victory was over course and distance. This was just one of those races, as TRADE WIND led near the post to beat CONSPICUOUS, neither having won a handicap before.

28 July NEWMARKET (Race 2746 6f Good to firm)

| 504200 | CZARNA | 4-10-0 | NWH |
| 010600 | SASEEDO | 5-10-0 | D |
| 005004 | SEA-DEER | 6-9-13 | H |
| 0-01462 | PRINCESS OBERON | 5-9-12 | H |
| 21104- | IKAAB | 3-9-9 | NWH |
| 116-304 | PENGAMON | 3-9-6 | NWH |
| 11100- | BELLO GALLICO | 4-9-3 | D |
| 4150-04 | CUMBRIAN WALTZER | 10-9-2 | D |
| 0-00201 | DRY POINT | 9-8-13 | C/D |
| 0-51442 | COOL EDGE | 4-8-13 | D |
| 010300 | BAYIN | 6-8-8 | D |
| 200031 | MISS ARAGON | 7-7-7 | C/D |

12 runners

# How to Beat the Handicapper

## C/D winners

DRY POINT same race 1994. Now 5lb higher, at 72, he had won at Kempton last time out off 69. However, he was now 9 years old, and his highest previous winning mark (73) was in July 1990. It is unlikely that he would be quite so good now. This was a difficult decision: I thought that he could be discounted, but would not be a false-priced favourite.

MISS ARAGON 7/95. Had won with a late finish - but in a slow time. In this system, a slow time can be ignored, except in handicaps of the highest class.

## D winners

BAYIN 5/95 Newbury. Held by the Handicapper.

BELLO GALLICO 4/94 Newmarket Rowley mile. If the going was good to soft, this would be a dark horse. He had won well for Richard Hannon, but then raced only twice more in 1994. I wondered if his new trainer, Lady Herries, could do something with him, but the going was very much against him.

COOL EDGE 5/94 Nottingham. Not won a handicap this season.

CUMBRIAN WALTZER 7/94 Ayr. Not won this season.

SASEEDO 5/95 Newmarket Rowley mile. Held by the Handicapper.

Selection: MISS ARAGON.    Challengers: BELLO GALLICO (if the going was soft; in which case MISS ARAGON would not be a selection).

After two disappointing runs over 5f at Newcastle and this course, PRINCESS OBERON was being tried at a new trip. This seemed a reasonable ploy for her trainer to adopt, but there was no reason for the punters to follow suit by making her a 5-1 favourite. MISS ARAGON was perhaps lucky enough to find another race slow enough to allow her to appear late and fast to win.

PRINCESS OBERON did not stay the extra furlong, and DRY POINT did not stay the pace. MISS ARAGON was entered for the hat-trick on 4th August, but was withdrawn just before the race.

5 August NEWMARKET (Race 2948 7f Good to firm)

| | | | |
|---|---|---|---|
| 2-52541 | KAYVEE | 6-10-0 | H |
| 411000 | CELESTIAL KEY | 5-9-11 | D |
| 6150021 | CADEAUX TRYST | 3-9-7 | C/D |
| 041221 | HI NOD | 5-9-3 | D |
| 12613/6 | RAMBO'S HALL | 10-9-1 | H |
| -32130 | CYRANO'S LAD | 6-9-0 | NWH |
| 23-10 | VERZEN | 3-8-13 | NWH |
| 506043 | GYMCRAK PREMIERE | 7-8-9 | H |
| 002155 | TAWAFIJ | 6-8-8 | D |
| 2000-02 | ABSOLUTE MAGIC | 5-8-8 | H |
| 004500 | MY BEST VALENTINE | 5-8-7 | D |
| 000-31 | FIRST VEIL | 5-8-3 | D |

0216-02   ELITE HOPE                 3-8-2     NWH

13 runners

After analysing the race, I had a strong intuition about both the selection and a false-priced favourite. Both proved as equally fallacious as when I had intuitions that my selection would win! My expectations were heightened by the fact the 7f July course has provided some very good results in the past.

## C/D winners

CADEAUX TRYST 7/95. Won the Bunbury Cup last time out, same going.

## D winners

CELESTIAL KEY 6/95 Newbury. Held by CADEAUX TRYST, in the Bunbury Cup.

HI NOD 7/95 Newcastle. Probably outclassed here, but could not be discounted.

MY BEST VALENTINE 6/94 Epsom. Not won this season.

TAWAFIJ 7/95 Newcastle. Only won on a disqualification, so effectively not won this season.

After reading Mark Winstanley's column in the *Sporting Life*, I hoped that VERZEN would be favourite. VERZEN had won a four-runner conditions stakes at Redcar on 30 May, and then been swamped in the Britannia Handicap (1m) at Royal Ascot. A great fan of VERZEN's trainer, D R Loder, Winstanley argued that 7f was the right distance. That might well be, but I could not see how he could be made favourite to win against some good handicappers.

CADEAUX TRYST appeared wearing bandages, as he had in his previous race, but perhaps this time it was serious: he trailed home last but one, while VERZEN ran on powerfully at the finish to win well.

## Selection: CADEAUX TRYST.          Challengers: HI NOD.

13 August LEOPARDSTOWN (7f Good to firm)

| | | | |
|---|---|---|---|
| 306501 | LADIES GALLERY | 5-9-11 | D |
| 300-051 | LOVING CONTRACT | 3-9-7 | C/D |
| 005606 | REGAL DOMAIN | 4-9-5 | C/D |
| 32-3140 | SAVING BOND | 3-9-3 | NWH |
| -22450 | VIKING DREAM | 3-9-1 | NWH |
| 0-41603 | AINE'S PET | 4-9-0 | H |
| 120033 | GLENISTA | 3-9-0 | D |
| 0-00006 | LOUGHMOGUE | 5-8-11 | NWR |
| -044 | BARBARA CADABRA | 3-8-9 | NWR |
| 600300 | HOLDERS HILL | 3-8-3 | NWR |

10 runners

This was the first selection in Ireland, perhaps because the 'greenhouse effect' was operating even there, and the going had been good or good to firm throughout the season.

# How to Beat the Handicapper

### C/D winners

LOVING CONTRACT 7/95. Won last time out.

REGAL DOMAIN 6/94. Not won this season.

### D winners

GLENISTA 4/95 Gowran Park. Held by LOVING CONTRACT.

LADIES GALLERY 8/95 Galway. Only won on soft going.

This was an averagely competitive race for Irish racing. LOVING CONTRACT won well last time out, and it seemed reasonable to expect that he could beat GLENISTA. In this case, GLENISTA would be a clear false-priced favourite.

The result was disappointing, as GLENISTA was 5-1 favourite, and LOVING CONTRACT was at a good price of 6-1. The race was won by the unconsidered BARBARA CADABRA.

### Selection: LOVING CONTRACT.    Challengers: None.

19 August THE CURRAGH (7f Good to firm)

| | | | |
|---|---|---|---|
| 010213 | BAYDUR | 4-9-13 | C/D |
| 01-10 | DARYBAD | 3-9-10 | NWH |
| 022321 | AILLEACHT | 3-9-9 | H |
| -3324 | DIAMOND CLASS | 5-9-7 | NWR |
| 3125-00 | TIRMIZI | 4-9-5 | NWH |
| 605126 | GER'S ROYALE | 4-9-1 | H |
| 221144 | MEGLIO CHE POSSO | 4-8-13 | H |
| 614004 | TAAJREH | 3-8-12 | NWH |
| 521510 | LIFE SUPPORT | 3-8-10 | D |
| 110231 | SUBARASHII | 4-8-10 | H |
| 0-03006 | MODEL SHOW | 4-8-9 | C/D |
| 056-62 | REGAL DOMAIN | 4-8-1 | NWH |
| 13030-5 | NABEEL | 9-7-10 | H |
| 000060 | LOUGHMOGUE | 5-7-7 | NWH |

14 runners

Throughout August, the going continued to remain good to firm in Ireland. Here was another opportunity, over a specialists' distance.

### C/D winners

BAYDUR 7/95. After his win here, on good to firm, ran over 6f. Now returns to course and distance.

MODEL SHOW 7/94. Not won this season.

### D winners

LIFE SUPPORT 7/95 Tipperary. Only won a fillies race.

# How to Beat the Handicapper

<u>Selection</u>: BAYDUR.                    <u>Challengers</u>: None.

Another averagely competitive race, with BAYDUR, trained by D K Weld, having a strong chance. Newspaper comment suggested that DIAMOND CLASS could reverse the form with BAYDUR given the change in the weights. He would have been a false-priced favourite, but BAYDUR went off a clear 3-1 favourite.

GER'S ROYALE, a handicap winner but only at 6f, won in the end, with BAYDUR somewhere in the ruck.

25 August THIRSK (Race 3357 5f Good to firm)

| | | | |
|---|---|---|---|
| 0600-06 | LOVELY ME | 4-10-0 | NWR |
| 20546-0 | SILK COTTAGE | 3-9-12 | NWH |
| 254005 | MISS MOVIE WORLD | 6-9-7 | D |
| 530265 | MOST UPPITTY | 3-9-2 | NWH |
| 000520 | INVIGILATE | 6-9-1 | D |
| 113003 | DOMINELLE | 3-8-11 | D |
| 40210 | KALAR | 6-8-10 | C/D |
| 05304 | KABCAST | 10-8-10 | C/D |
| -655 | SELF STYLED | 3-8-9 | NWH |
| 450060 | THE INSTITUTE BOY | 5-8-8 | NWH |
| 630025 | ABLE SHERIFF | 3-8-8 | NWH |
| 056244 | MURRAY'S MAZDA | 6-8-3 | NWH |
| 040-0 | CHARDONNAY GIRL | 4-8-1 | NWR |
| 000306 | INDIAN CRYSTAL | 4-7-11 | NWR |
| 0-065 | LADYS PROMISE | 3-7-7 | NWR |
| 00030 | CONEY HILLS | 4-7-7 | NWR |

16 runners

As in most seasons, there was something of a lull for most of August, at least as far as British racing was concerned. This seems to be a natural pause in the rhythm of the Flat programme, and it is not until the end of August that the momentum is resumed. At this relatively late stage in the game, it seemed unlikely that there would be a handicap in which over half the runners had either not won a handicap or a race - but here it was.

## C/D winners

KALAR 8/93 same race 1993. A perfect illustration of the vagaries of the handicap system. He had won the same race off 45; had won a 5f handicap at Catterick on 1 August (Race 2837); been well beaten off 47 beaten at an unsuitable course (Leicester); and was still on a reasonable mark, 47, only 2lb higher than his 1993 win.

KABCAST 8/91. Not won this season.

## D winners

MISS MOVIE WORLD 8/94 Redcar. Not won this season.

INVIGILATE 7/92 Sandown. Not won since 1992.

DOMINELLE 7/95 Carlisle. Held by KALAR at Catterick.

<u>Selection</u>: KALAR.                    <u>Challengers</u>: None.

# How to Beat the Handicapper

It is true that INVIGILATE had seen much better days, at Sandown, but these were very much in the past. Why he should be a joint-favourite with KALAR was very much a mystery, making him a definite false-priced favourite. In the, race he was only just caught in the last stride, by KALAR.

26 August NEWCASTLE (Race 3368 1m Good to firm)

| | | | |
|---|---|---|---|
| 4-22113 | HAKIKA | 3-10-0 | D |
| 431-13 | CRUMPTON HILL | 3-10-0 | D |
| 013015 | CLIFTON FOX | 3-9-2 | D |
| 610535 | DESERT TIME | 5-9-12 | D |
| 541023 | KEMO SABO | 3-9-9 | D |
| 05-0312 | ALMOND ROCK | 3-9-7 | D |
| -2210-0 | CURRENT SPEECH | 4-9-7 | NWH |
| 212124 | SHINEROLLA | 3-9-5 | D |
| 0-05003 | FOREVER DIAMONDS | 8-9-5 | D |
| 0-13111 | SCARABEN | 7-8-11 | C/D |
| 31441 | THATCHED | 5-8-4 | D |
| 622402 | MARY'S CASE | 5-8-2 | NWH |
| 461060 | MAROWINS | 6-7-8 | D |

13 runners

At first glance, despite being only a Class D handicap, with a top weight rated 85, this seemed to be one of the most competitive handicaps I had analysed, with 11 distance winners out of 13 runners. A closer look, after a good half hour, showed that there was an outstanding selection.

## C/D winners

SCARABEN 6/95. Won last time out. *Reflections on Running* had reported that he had won that race in 'most decisive' fashion - quite an accolade. His 3lb claimer had won on him previously.

## D winners

ALMOND ROCK 7/95 Salisbury. Beaten one and a quarter lengths off 76, she was now on 78. Held by the Handicapper.

CLIFTON FOX 5/95 Leicester. As he had only run once since, he could not be discounted.

CRUMPTON HILL 5/95 Newbury. Held off this mark.

DESERT TIME 8/95 Goodwood. Held off this mark.

FOREVER DIAMONDS 5/94 Haydock. Not won this season.

HAKIKA 7/95 Beverley. Only a five-runner race.

KEMO SABO 7/95 Ayr. Held off 72, now off 80. Held by the Handicapper.

MAROWINS 6/95 Thirsk. Held off this mark.

# How to Beat the Handicapper

SHINEROLLA 5/95 Pontefract. Stayed on well into fourth, beaten four lengths, off 72, now 76. Held by the Handicapper.

THATCHED 8/95 Carlisle. Won by eight lengths, can not be discounted.

Selection: SCARABEN.    Challengers: CLIFTON FOX; THATCHED.

The false-priced favourite came from an unexpected source. *'Man on the Spot'* (*Sporting Life*) argued that his '...close second to FIONN DE COOL suggests he's not handicapped out of it yet.' Apart from being trained by Reg Akehurst (in itself, a considerable plus), FIONN DE COOL was no big deal - after beating ALMOND ROCK, he was easily held in his next race.
 SCARABEN won in pretty good style, always keeping THATCHED in second place.

27 August TRALEE (1m 4f Good to firm)

| | | | |
|---|---|---|---|
| 10-2343 | OZETTE | 4-10-0 | NWH |
| 123321 | MAGIC FEELING | 5-9-11 | C/D |
| 20155S | DIAMOND DISPLAY | 4-8-13 | H |
| 0514-00 | SALMON RIVER | 4-8-12 | NWH |
| 00-0000 | WESBEST | 6-8-12 | D |
| 32-2106 | WAFIR | 3-8-9 | NWH |
| 002113 | KAKASHDA | 4-8-6 | D |
| 4-02021 | BELLE DE CADIX | 3-8-0 | NWH |
| 4-03465 | TABBASSAM | 3-7-13 | NWR |

9 runners

Even on the west coast, the going remained firm. This was an irritating state of affairs for Irish trainers, who usually have a lot of soft ground performers in their stables, but it did not seem to reduce the number of handicap opportunities at this stage of the season.

## C/D winners

MAGIC FEELING same race 1994. Won well last time out over 1m 4f at Leopardstown.

## D winners

KAKASHDA 8/95 Galway. Recently won 2 handicaps over the distance, his last run (in a Listed race) could be ignored, so he could not be discounted.

WESBEST 7/93 Galway. Not won since July 1993.

Selection: MAGIC FEELING.    Challengers: KAKASHDA.

KAKASHDA was a reasonable favourite at 9-4, but was well held by MAGIC FEELING, trained by the irrepressible Aidan O'Brien.

8 September DONCASTER (Race 3597 5f Good to soft)

| | | | |
|---|---|---|---|
| 010026 | ANN'S PEARL | 4-10-0 | D |
| 014230 | BEAU VENTURE | 7-9-13 | D |
| 106566- | POLLY PARTICULAR | 3-9-12 | NWH |

| 2-22110 | BROADSTAIRS BEAUTY | 5-9-11 | D |
|---------|--------------------|--------|-----|
| 20-5400 | THICK AS THIEVES | 3-9-10 | NWH |
| 011225 | LADY SHERIFF | 4-9-10 | D |
| 413410 | HERE COMES A STAR | 7-9-8 | D |
| 22060 | SHADOW JURY | 5-9-7 | D |
| 65-6660 | SOUND THE TRUMPET | 3-9-7 | NWH |
| -1016 | GENERAL SIR PETER | 3-9-5 | C/D |
| 00-0300 | BOLD STREET | 5-9-6 | D |
| 415246 | BOLLIN HARRY | 3-9-3 | D |
| 342213 | NITE-OWL DANCER | 3-9-3 | D |
| 042525 | JUST BOB | 6-9-2 | D |
| 224100 | JUST DISSIDENT | 3-9-1 | NWH |
| 026324 | CAPTAIN CARAT | 4-9-0 | H |
| 001- | KUNG FRODE | 3-8-12 | NWR |

17 runners

Another Class D handicap, only this time it *looked* difficult, but appearances were equally - and even more rewardingly - deceptive. The favourite was even more falsely priced.

## C/D winners

GENERAL SIR PETER 7/95. I discounted as being irrelevant his only race (Race 3219 28 August Sandown 5f) since winning over course and distance.

## D winners

ANN'S PEARL 5/95 Bath. Held by the Handicapper.

BEAU VENTURE 6/95 Ripon. Held by the Handicapper.

BOLD STREET 4/94 Sandown. Not won this season.

BOLLIN HARRY 6/95 Catterick. Held by LADY SHERIFF, 22 July Newcastle.

BROADSTAIRS BEAUTY 7/95 Newmarket. His one subsequent run, in the ultra-competitive Stewards' Cup at Goodwood, can be ignored, so he can not be discounted.

HERE COMES A STAR 8/95 Carlisle. Unsuited by the softer going.

JUST BOB 8/94 Carlisle. Not won this season.

LADY SHERIFF 7/95 York. Held by the Handicapper.

NITE-OWL DANCER 8/95 Redcar. Had only win against fillies.

SHADOW JURY 7/95 Ayr Held by the Handicapper.

Selection: GENERAL SIR PETER. Challengers: BROADSTAIRS BEAUTY

I wonder how many punters will say 'Thank God for the Ramsdens!' But I do - not so much for the Ramsdens, an enviable combination of a very capable trainer (Mrs) and an astute backer (Mr), but for the journalists who attempt to second-guess their motives, as a source of easy copy. CAPTAIN CARAT was made 4-1 favourite here, on the basis that he 'likes Doncaster' (which is true - but over 6f) and had that he had 'run well' over 5f ('admittedly heavy going') - today's going was no more than good to soft.

There were the inevitable hard luck stories after CAPTAIN CARAT had been bumped at the start, and had 'met all sorts of trouble' (the usually perceptive *Raceform*). GENERAL SIR PETER pipped LADY SHERIFF at the post, but really without much difficulty.

8 September GOODWOOD (Race 3615 6f Good)

| | | | |
|---|---|---|---|
| 00651 | NO EXTRAS | 5-10-0 | C/D |
| 621411 | IKTAMAL | 3-9-12 | D |
| 0-50041 | CROESO-I-CYMRU | 4-9-8 | NWH |
| 6430202 | HOW'S YER FATHER | 9-9-3 | C/D |
| -1532 | PENNY DIP | 3-9-0 | NWH |
| 2-31203 | HAKIKI | 3-9-0 | NWH |
| 3-22315 | SEA THUNDER | 3-8-11 | NWH |
| 312050 | THATCHERELLA | 4-8-9 | D |
| 001100 | CHAMPAGNE GRANDY | 5-8-9 | D |
| 060252 | BAJAN ROSE | 3-8-6 | NWH |
| 632060 | AGWA | 6-8-6 | D |
| 4-05005 | MONTSERRAT | 3-8-5 | NWH |
| 320660 | JATO | 6-8-5 | D |
| 240124 | ANZIO | 4-8-4 | H |
| 5-20502 | SUE ME | 3-8-2 | D |
| 513050 | LA PETITE FUSEE | 4-8-2 | D |
| 224502 | RICH GLOW | 4-8-1 | H |
| 630000- | FASCINATION WALTZ | 8-8-1 | D |
| 0-41042 | DANCING HEART | 3-8-0 | H |
| 023104 | OGGI | 4-8-0 | D |
| 025504 | GONE SAVAGE | 7-7-12 | D |
| 152364 | TINKER OSMASTON | 4-7-12 | H |
| 002106 | PETRACO | 7-7-11 | D |
| 000436 | ASTRAL INVADER | 3-7-7 | NWH |
| 000005 | GREEN GOLIGHTLY | 4-7-7 | D |
| 006000 | CRAIGIE BOY | 5-7-7 | D |

26 runners

This race also looked insoluble. It was not - only the solution was wrong!

## C/D winners

NO EXTRAS 8/95. Last time out.
HOW'S YER FATHER 6/93. Not won since June 1993.

## D winners

AGWA 4/94 Salisbury. Not won this season.

CHAMPAGNE GRANDY 6/95 Salisbury. Can not be discounted.

CRAIGIE BOY 4/94 Hamilton. Not won this season.

FASCINATION WALTZ 6/93. Not won this season.

GONE SAVAGE 4/95 Kempton. Held off this mark.

GREEN GOLIGHTLY 6/94 Windsor. Not won this season.

IKTAMAL 8/95 Haydock. Can not be discounted.

JATO 7/94 Pontefract. Not won this season.

LA PETITE FUSEE 6/95 Lingfield. Held off this mark.

OGGI 5/95 Newbury. Can not be discounted.

PETRACO 7/93 Warwick. Held by NO EXTRAS last time out.

SUE ME 10/94 York. Not won this season.

THATCHERELLA 5/95 Chepstow. Held by the Handicapper.

Selection: NO EXTRAS.    Challengers: CHAMPAGNE GRANDY; IKTAMAL; OGGI.

IKTAMAL could not be faulted as market leader, at 8-1, since he had good recent form. Faced with three valid challengers, and a field of 26 runners, NO EXTRAS was at a quite legitimate price of 14-1.

Although IKTAMAL won after leading inside the final furlong, NO EXTRAS was not disgraced by being fourth, beaten less than a length. However, he was unable to go with the early pace, and for the future I thought that he was definitely held off this mark. The Handicapper did not agree and raised him 1lb.

In this case, the Handicapper's judgement was excellent, for in his next race, the highly competitive 6f Gold Cup at Ayr (Race 3717 16 September), NO EXTRAS ran on well to be beaten only by a neck. By the end of the season, after losing three more races, he had reached a mark of 102.

13 September GALWAY (1m 100y Good to firm)

| | | | |
|---|---|---|---|
| 10-5130 | TRIGGER HAPPY JOHN | 4-10-0 | H |
| 13-0132 | JAKDUL | 4-9-13 | NWH |
| 241-644 | BLITZER | 3-9-9 | H |
| 1-36343 | HOLIWAY STAR | 5-9-9 | H |
| -4135 | YAVANA'S PACE | 3-9-9 | H |
| 065010 | LADIES GALLERY | 5-9-7 | H |
| -521 | PROPAGANDA COUP | 3-9-7 | NWH |
| 120410 | FRASER CAREY | 3-9-6 | NWH |
| 0641- | PEACE PROCESS | 3-9-6 | NWH |
| 141010 | GLASDERRYMORE | 3-9-4 | C/D |
| 00- | DAKARNA | 5-9-1 | NWH |
| 451122 | MONICA'S CHOICE | 4-9-0 | H |
| 314040 | SAVING BOND | 3-9-0 | NWH |
| 265360 | BE MY FOLLY | 3-8-10 | NWH |
| 00-1040 | PHARDY | 4-8-8 | C/D |
| -0006 | LEGAL DRAMA | 3-8-0 | NWR |
| -065 | MIXED PINT | 3-8-0 | NWR |

| 600500  | ALBERTA ROSE | 6-7-7 | H   |
| 000540- | CANGERAC     | 4-7-7 | NWR |

19 runners

## C/D winners

GLASDERRYMORE 8/95. His performance in the only race after the course and distance victory, a Listed stakes, could be discounted.

PHARDY 9/94 apprentice. Not won a handicap this season.

## D winners

None.

## Selection: GLASDERRYMORE.          Challengers: None.

As I say in chapter 4, a horse trained by Dermot Weld running in a handicap after winning a stakes does have a good chance, and, exceptionally, is not a false-priced favourite. PROPAGANDA COUP was a well backed 7-2 favourite in this race. The selection, GLASDERRYMORE, was never in with a chance behind the winner, YAVANA'S PACE.

25 September HAMILTON (Race 3852 1m 4f 17y Good to firm)

| 001404  | NO COMEBACKS     | 7-9-12 | D   |
| 142323  | MENTALASANYTHIN  | 6-9-12 | C/D |
| 00-0255 | CUTTHROAT KID    | 5-9-11 | C/D |
| 111010  | PHARLY DANCER    | 6-9-4  | D   |
| 001264  | AYUNLI           | 4-9-1  | NWH |
| 304501  | CHANTRY BEATH    | 4-8-13 | C/D |
| 311240  | LORD HASTIE      | 7-8-11 | D   |
| 0-00050 | PENDOLINO        | 4-8-9  | H   |
| 306123  | DIAMOND CROWN    | 4-8-8  | NWH |
| 450605  | KEEP BATTLING    | 5-8-1  | H   |
| 055003  | ACHILLES HEEL    | 4-8-1  | D   |
| 060160  | KINOKO           | 7-7-13 | D   |
| 000-60  | STORMLESS        | 4-7-11 | NWR |
| 434310  | LORD ADVOCATE    | 7-7-10 | D   |
| 350640  | KANAT LEE        | 4-7-7  | NWH |
| 60U0-05 | KALKO            | 6-7-7  | NWH |

16 runners

By comparison with the cracking start in April and May, September and October went out very tamely indeed. Perhaps this was because of the unusually fine weather in the last two months of the season. Even in Scotland there was a heat wave, and the going at Ayr and Hamilton, usually boggy at this date, was unseasonably firm.

## C/D winners

CHANTRY BEATH 7/94. Won last time out at Edinburgh, and in good form.

CUTTHROAT KID 9/94. Not won this season.

# How to Beat the Handicapper

MENTALASANYTHIN same race 1994. Put back in distance from most recent win.

## D winners

ACHILLES HEEL 3/95 Doncaster apprentice. Held by CHANTRY BEATH last time out.

KINOKO 7/95 Beverley, 5 runners. Held by the Handicapper.

LORD ADVOCATE 8/95 Edinburgh. Held by CHANTRY BEATH last time out.

LORD HASTIE 7/95 Ripon. Can not be discounted.

NO COMEBACKS 7/95 Chester. Can not be discounted.

PHARLY DANCER 4/95 Catterick. Held by the Handicapper.

Selection: CHANTRY BEATH.       Challengers: LORD HASTIE; NO COMEBACKS.

CHANTRY BEATH was the warm favourite, at 3-1. This was explicable enough, but not so the winner, AYUNLI. Who? Her name may have featured prominently on the following Sunday, in sermons on the folly of gambling, but to readers of the form book, who she? If this had been the first race I had ever analysed along the lines set out in this book, I would not have gone any further, but would have given up straight away.

2 October PONTEFRACT (Race 3973 8f 4y Good to firm)

| | | | |
|---|---|---|---|
| 131533 | NORDINEX | 3-9-7 | D |
| 0-0310 | ROSEBERRY RAY | 3-9-5 | D |
| -160 | MARGUERITE BAY | 3-9-5 | NWH |
| 212400 | SHINEROLLA | 3-9-4 | C/D |
| 401003 | ELPIDOS | 3-9-4 | D |
| -321 | FAR AHEAD | 3-9-3 | NWH |
| 006350 | FORZAIR | 3-8-11 | NWR |
| -003 | ALZOOMO | 3-8-10 | NWR |
| 203246 | SEVENTEENS LUCKY | 3-8-10 | NWR |
| 263610 | THREE ARCH BRIDGE | 3-8-7 | H |
| 535056 | EVAN 'ELP US | 3-8-3 | NWR |
| 413256 | ELITE RACING | 3-8-4 | D |
| -00455 | TRUE BALLAD | 3-8-2 | NWR |
| 05-0050 | EL DON | 3-7-10 | NWR |
| 032602 | SHINING EDGE | 3-7-9 | NWR |

15 runners

Even though this did not seem much of a race, with seven maidens and two non-handicap winners, rules are rules and had to be applied here.

## C/D winners

SHINEROLLA 5/95. Seems held by the Handicapper; over 90 days since last win.

## D winners

ELITE RACING 5/95 Brighton. Well beaten last time out. Held off this mark.

ELPIDOS 8/95 Sandown. Held off this mark.

NORDINEX 7/95 Newmarket. Held off this mark.

ROSEBERRY RAY 8/95 Hamilton. Beaten in only subsequent race, over 1m 2f at Yarmouth. Can not be discounted.

SHINEROLLA had been running in much better company, and was now back to a course and distance where he had won easily in May. Mrs Ramsden had publicly stated her intention of giving him a break in the middle of the season, and bringing him back for an autumn campaign. This was it - but however weak the rest of the field looked, SHINEROLLA had not won since 26 May, and was discounted.

## Selection: None.

Even though he was running off a mark 9lb higher than in May, SHINEROLLA won this race rather smoothly. Performing creditably in a Newmarket handicap on his next and final outing (Race 4116 14 October), his Pontefract days are probably over - at least for a year or two.

21 October DONCASTER (Race 4197 5f Good to firm)

| | | | |
|---|---|---|---|
| 311140 | THAT MAN AGAIN | 3-9-7 | D |
| 244143 | COFFEE 'N CREAM | 3-9-2 | D |
| 051032 | TAKADOU | 4-8-13 | D |
| 220011 | CROFT POOL | 4-8-10 | D |
| 101000 | NAME THE TUNE | 4-8-10 | C/D |
| 060440 | CALL ME I'M BLUE | 5-8-8 | D |
| 600605 | ZIGGY'S DANCER | 4-8-8 | H |
| 000000 | ASHTINA | 10-8-7 | D |
| 0536-00 | SEIGNEURIAL | 3-8-6 | NWH |
| 562104 | THE HAPPY FOX | 3-8-6 | NWH |

10 runners

An average British Flat season ended in a distinctly unusual way, with only one selection in October. The final race worked out almost entirely to form, the 'almost' being the selection!

## C/D winners

NAME THE TUNE 3/94. After winning at Sandown on 19 August, he had run in the Portland Handicap (Doncaster 5f 140y), the Gold Cup (Ayr 6f), and on soft going at Ascot (5f). This seemed a good opportunity.

## D winners

ASHTINA 5/95 Chester. Held by CROFT POOL last time out.

CALL ME I'M BLUE 9/93. Not won since 1993

COFFEE 'N CREAM 8/95 Ascot. Last two runs over 6f: can not be discounted.

CROFT POOL 10/95 Newmarket. Can not be discounted.

# How to Beat the Handicapper

TAKADOU 8/94 Newmarket. Held by CROFT POOL.

THAT MAN AGAIN 8/95 Haydock. Held off this mark.

Selection: NAME THE TUNE.    Challengers: COFFEE 'N CREAM; CROFT POOL.

CROFT POOL was a reasonable favourite at 7-2, but it was hard to see the joint favourite, TAKADOU, reversing the form. Given that he had been running in much more competitive races, NAME THE TUNE seemed to be in with a chance at 13-2.

In a blanket finish, CROFT POOL held on by half a length from COFFEE 'N CREAM, with NAME THE TUNE, unable to recover ground lost at the start, another half-length and two necks away in fifth.

24 October REDCAR (Race 4236 7f Firm)

| | | | |
|---|---|---|---|
| 24-5006 | NEW CENTURY | 3-10-0 | NWH |
| 121000 | KING RAT | 4-9-10 | C/D |
| -3212 | FAR AHEAD | 3-9-7 | NWH |
| 651360 | PARLIAMENT PIECE | 9-9-4 | C/D |
| 524310 | QUILLING | 3-9-2 | C/D |
| 0-14600 | GLOWING JADE | 5-9-1 | D |
| 1-02300 | SUPERPRIDE | 3-9-1 | NWH |
| 222510 | KID ORY | 4-9-1 | C/D |
| 3652/06 | FIELD OF VISION | 5-8-10 | C/D |
| 400000 | SUPER PARK | 3-8-9 | NWH |
| 312200 | SUPER BENZ | 9-8-7 | C/D |
| 260422 | MISTER WESTSOUND | 3-8-6 | H |
| 100000 | PENNY'S WISHING | 3-7-12 | NWH |
| 0020-30 | ALABANG | 4-7-9 | NWH |
| 600050 | MU-ARRIK | 7-7-7 | H |

15 runners

This race was analysed for the record, as part of assessing whether the Redcar 7f was suited to course and distance specialists. It was an interesting race in its own right, as it is not very often that there are six course and distance winners, and only one distance winner.

## C/D winners

FIELD OF VISION 6/93. Not won since 1993.
KID ORY 9/95. Won last course and distance race 'just held on'. Only won on good going.

KING RAT 8/95. Held by KID ORY last time over course and distance.

PARLIAMENT PIECE 7/94. Not won a handicap this season.

QUILLING 10/95. In only subsequent race, unplaced at Haydock over 6f, good to soft, a run which could be safely ignored.

SUPER BENZ 10/91. Not won this season.

## D winners

GLOWING JADE 5/95 Doncaster apprentice. Discount, as only won an apprentice handicap this season, over 90 days ago.

If this had already been shown to be a suitable course and distance, QUILLING would clearly have been a selection, with no challengers. In this race, there was a classic false-priced favourite, as MISTER WESTSOUND was backed from 8-1 to 9-2 to reverse the form with QUILLING.

QUILLING won the race easily enough, with MISTER WESTSOUND well beaten.

28 October LEOPARDSTOWN (1m 2f Good)

| | | | |
|---|---|---|---|
| 600506 | OH'CECILIA | 3-10-0 | H |
| 144055 | MEGLIO CHE POSSO | 4-9-13 | H |
| 602-560 | NEVER BACK DOWN | 5-9-10 | NWH |
| 043311 | SILVIAN BLISS | 3-9-9 | H |
| 4-60061 | MOY WATER | 3-9-8 | NWH |
| 613646 | ZALARA | 3-9-8 | D |
| 220234 | STREET VIEW | 3-9-7 | NWH |
| 531220 | CHAMPAGNE HURLEY | 4-9-6 | H |
| 30-0013 | GRACEFUL RESIGN | 4-9-6 | NWH |
| 16-3000 | PROSAIC STAR | 3-9-4 | NWH |
| 1104-50 | EUPHORIC | 4-9-2 | NWH |
| 231301 | SPARKLY GIRL | 4-9-1 | H |
| 130130 | SOFT SPOT | 3-8-13 | C/D |
| 35061-3 | BANK STATEMENT | 4-8-12 | NWH |
| 051002 | LEGGAGH LADY | 4-8-12 | NWH |
| 202004 | DESERT CALM | 6-8-10 | NWH |
| 603455 | BENE MERENTI | 5-8-8 | H |
| 423043 | PORT QUEEN | 4-8-4 | H |
| 020006 | SAMINA | 3-8-4 | NWH |
| 0-00502 | PEIRSEACH | 3-8-0 | NWR |
| 5-02100 | BAJAN QUEEN | 5-7-12 | H |
| 022103 | KESS | 6-7-9 | D |

22 runners

## C/D winners

SOFT SPOT 9/95. Ran in two unsuitable races, and is now back over course and distance. Won on good and good to firm.

## D winners

KESS 9/95 Clonmel. Won on good, good-yielding. Can not be discounted.

ZALARA 7/95 Roscommon. Held by the Handicapper.

Selection: SOFT SPOT (if suitable going).          Challengers: KESS.

Very much depended on the going, as SOFT SPOT was an unknown quantity on yielding, the going forecast by the *Sporting Life*. At the time of the off, however, the going was good.

As the *Irish Field* stated after the event, something happened that was not known in 'modern times': no SP's were reported, because the bookmakers refused to stand, in protest against the introduction of on-course betting shops. This was especially annoying, as the pre-race S.P. forecasts suggested that there was a strong possibility of a false-priced favourite, and that there was a good price against SOFT SPOT. All that we do know is that SOFT SPOT just got home - which was no consolation!

28 October NEWMARKET (Race 4267 1m Good to firm)

| | | | |
|---|---|---|---|
| 541000 | KAYVEE | 6-10-0 | D |
| 130211 | NIGHT DANCE | 3-9-7 | D |
| -0131 | TARAWA | 3-9-2 | C/D |
| 210310 | WEAVER BIRD | 5-9-2 | D |
| 6-04134 | SHARP REVIEW | 7-9-2 | H |
| 013132 | WESTERN FAME | 3-9-1 | H |
| 130413 | RON'S SECRET | 3-9-1 | D |
| 21100-0 | ETHBAAT | 4-9-1 | H |
| 46-104 | DELTA SOLEIL | 3-8-13 | NWH |
| 164000 | BILLY BUSHWACKER | 4-8-13 | D |
| 605501 | STONE RIDGE | 3-8-13 | C/D |
| 552600 | WAKEEL | 3-8-12 | NWH |
| 250131 | COMANCHE COMPANION | 5-8-11 | D |
| D43220 | BALL GOWN | 5-8-10 | D |
| 100064 | ERTLON | 5-8-10 | D |
| 322235 | COOL EDGE | 4-8-9 | H |
| 421012 | MO-ADDAB | 5-8-9 | D |
| 6-5000 | OUR RITA | 6-8-9 | D |
| 124050 | CELESTIAL CHOIR | 5-8-9 | D |
| 060020 | SERIOUS | 5-8-8 | NWH |
| 050205 | PAY HOMAGE | 7-8-8 | D |
| 00025 | COUNTRY LOVER | 4-8-7 | D |
| 221212 | CONSPICUOUS | 5-8-7 | H |
| 015504 | CLIFTON FOX | 3-8-6 | D |
| 225301 | SAMBA SHARPLY | 4-8-5 | D |
| -24102 | CELTIC FRINGE | 3-8-5 | NWH |
| 4-0233 | NOBLE SPRINTER | 3-8-5 | NWH |
| 501050 | MA PETITE ANGLAISE | 3-8-4 | D |
| 212100 | APPOLONO | 3-8-4 | D |
| 24100 | SAIFAN | 6-8-4 | C/D |

30 runners

The final race analysed here is to show what to do when comparing two course and distance winners: one which wins with a good late finish (analysed in my previous books); and the other, which is the subject of the system set out in this book.

The analysis set out below also shows that the system can make sense of one of the most daunting types of handicap in the calendar: an end-of-season race, with 30 runners, and a large number of qualifiers (3 course and distance winners, and 18 distance winners).

Weighing up the chances of 30 runners does take much more than the average 10 minutes required by the system. This race took 35 minutes to sort out, the longest time this season.

## C/D winners

SAIFAN 10/93. Held by STONE RIDGE.

STONE RIDGE 10/95. Won last time out: led 3f out, held on well.

TARAWA 10/95. Won last time out: accelerated at the distance, and ran on strongly.

## D winners

APOLLONO 7/95 Brighton. Held by STONE RIDGE.

BALL GOWN 9/94 Salisbury. Winning over longer distances.

BILLY BUSHWHACKER 3/95 Doncaster. Not won for over 90 days; held off this mark.

CELESTIAL CHOIR 8/95 won on a disqualification: not won this season.

CLIFTON FOX 5/95 Leicester. Held by STONE RIDGE.

COMANCHE COMPANION 8/94 Pontefract. Much better suited by good or good to soft.

COUNTRY LOVER 7/94 Salisbury. Held by STONE RIDGE.

ERTLON 8/93 York. Held off this mark.

KAYVEE 6/95 Ascot. Held off this mark.

MA PETITE ANGLAISE 7/95 Windsor. Held by STONE RIDGE.

MO-ADDAB 9/95 Ascot. Held by STONE RIDGE.

NIGHT DANCE 10/95 Ascot. Won last time out: Can not be discounted.

OUR RITA 3/94 Doncaster. Not won this season.

PAY HOMAGE 5/93 Sandown. Most recent win over 1m 1f: put back in distance.

RON'S SECRET 10/95 Haydock. Mark raised by 15lb for winning a three-runner handicap by three-quarters of a length.

SAMBA SHARPLY 10/95 Nottingham. Not won on an uphill finish.

WEAVER BIRD 8/95 Windsor. Has won on an uphill finish; one race after her Windsor victory, over 1m 1f. Can not be discounted.

STONE RIDGE conveniently holds five of the distance winners on the strength of their last race, over course and distance. If the only other course and distance winner were SAIFAN, he would be the selection. But TARAWA won much more impressively, accelerating with a strong late finish. He also has a story line - a lightly-raced three-year-old - and is trained by a handicap expert, Neville Callaghan. For these reasons, he was preferred over STONE RIDGE.

It was unlikely that there would be a false-priced favourite in such a strong field, but for a few minutes it seemed possible.

DELTA SOLEIL had not won a handicap, but won a York maiden impressively. The form looks less impressive when checked: the York race had only five runners, and his only two runs in handicap company were 8th (Race 3659 13 September Yarmouth 1m 2f 21y) and 4th (Race 3943 30 September Newmarket 7f). DELTA SOLEIL and NIGHT DANCE opened as joint favourites at 10-1, but then separated, to be 17-2 and 15-2 respectively.

In the race, NIGHT DANCE, STONE RIDGE and WEAVER BIRD all finished in mid-division, while TARAWA accelerated to another comfortable victory. DELTA SOLEIL challenged briefly at about the furlong pole, but he could not match strides with the winner.

## LIST OF SELECTIONS

FPF = false-priced favourite

### APRIL

| 5  | Ripon     | PALACEGATE TOUCH | W 9-1 | FPF |
|----|-----------|------------------|-------|-----|
| 18 | Newmarket | TUDOR ISLAND     | W 7-1 | FPF |
| 26 | Catterick | KINOKO           | L 7-1 |     |

### MAY

| 1  | Pontefract | OBELOS            | L 9-4 fav     |     |
|----|------------|-------------------|---------------|-----|
| 7  | Newmarket  | MASTER PLANNER    | W 9-1         |     |
| 12 | Beverley   | ROLLING THE BONES | W 11-10 fav   |     |
| 17 | York       | SADDLEHOME        | L 7-1         |     |
| 20 | Thirsk     | HI NOD            | L 6-1 jt-fav  |     |
| 22 | Bath       | VANBOROUGH LAD    | W 8-1         | FPF |
| 24 | Goodwood   | CASTLEREA LAD     | W 11-2        | FPF |
| 25 | Newcastle  | GOOD HAND         | W 4-1 jt-fav  |     |
| 27 | Haydock    | LORD HIGH ADMIRAL | W 10-1        | FPF |
| 29 | Doncaster  | MIDNIGHT JAZZ     | L 8-1         | FPF |
| 31 | Ripon      | THE SCYTHIAN      | W 10-1        | FPF |

### JUNE

| 2  | Bath      | INCHCAILLOCH       | W 4-1 jt-fav | FPF |
|----|-----------|--------------------|--------------|-----|
| 5  | Windsor   | SCENIC DANCER      | L 7-2 jt-fav |     |
| 7  | Warwick   | MYFONTAINE         | W 9-4 fav    |     |
| 14 | Beverley  | EURO SCEPTIC       | L 13-2       | FPF |
| 16 | Sandown   | SPECIAL DAWN       | W 9-4        | FPF |
| 17 | Sandown   | EMBRACING          | W 15-8 fav   |     |
| 20 | Thirsk    | LOOKINGFORARAINBOW | L 5-2 fav    |     |
| 30 | Newcastle | PRINCESS OBERON    | L 6-1        | FPF |

### JULY

| 2  | Doncaster | BETTERGETON | W 5-1     | FPF |
|----|-----------|-------------|-----------|-----|
| 6  | Catterick | MAC'S TAXI  | L 5-1     |     |
| 7  | Beverley  | COUREUR     | L 3-1 fav |     |
| 28 | Newmarket | MISS ARAGON | W 9-1     | FPF |

### AUGUST

| 5 | Newmarket | CADEAUX TRYST | L 7-1 | FPF |
|---|-----------|---------------|-------|-----|

| 13 | Leopardstown | LOVING CONTRACT | L 7-1 | FPF |
| 19 | The Curragh | BAYDUR | L 3-1 fav | |
| 25 | Thirsk | KALAR | W 5-1 jt-fav | FPF |
| 26 | Newcastle | SCARABEN | W 15-2 | FPF |
| 27 | Tralee | MAGIC FEELING | W 11-2 | |

## SEPTEMBER

| 8 | Doncaster | GENERAL SIR PETER | W 11-1 | FPF |
| 8 | Goodwood | NO EXTRAS | L 14-1 | |
| 13 | Galway | GLASDERRYMORE | L 12-1 | |
| 25 | Hamilton | CHANTRY BEATH | L 3-1 fav | |

## OCTOBER

| 21 | Doncaster | NAME THE TUNE | L 13-2 |
| 28 | Leopardstown | SOFT SPOT | W no SP |

38 races 20 winners (53% strike-rate).

## LIST OF NON-SELECTION RACES

These races were included to illustrate one of the system's principles (given in brackets).

## MAY

16 York ROGER THE BUTLER
(same race winner running off a higher mark)

## JUNE

12 Warwick MYFONTAINE
(weight exceeding 10st)

16 York SAINT EXPRESS
(not won a handicap this season)

## JULY

17 Windsor DR. EDGAR/ JUST FLAMENCO
(two course and distance winners with equal chances)

## OCTOBER

2 Pontefract SHINEROLLA
(held by the Handicapper; 90 day rule)

24 Redcar QUILLING
(recording a new course and distance)
28 Newmarket STONE RIDGE/TARAWA

# How to Beat the Handicapper

(course and distance winner meets a late flier - in this system, two with equal chances)

The results for this season also show that you must be prepared to take the long-term view. In terms of general cases:

1. two of the best courses from the point of view of this system are Beverley and Leicester. Yet in 1995, the results were dreadful at Beverley (1 short-priced winner and 2 losers) and non-existent at Leicester (no selections at all).

2. one of the best distances, 7f, indeed a 'specialist distance' in itself, produced five losers, by a long way the worst of the last ten seasons. HI NOD won three 7f races, but the only time he ran at the 'right' course and distance, he lost!

3. the table, LIST OF NON-SELECTION RACES, set out above, reports a 40% strike-rate in this kind of race which was representative of the season as a whole, whereas the average seasonal strike-rate is much nearer 25%.

Finally, in specific cases, there was one unusual accident in running (when LOOKINGFORARAINBOW hit the rails, Race 1844 20 June Thirsk) and what the bookmakers would have called 'an unusual betting pattern' - except for the fact that there was no betting at all, in the race won by SOFT SPOT at Leopardstown on 28 October 1995.

On the credit side, the season was not statistically exceptional. The overall strike-rate of all selections was 53% (slightly above the ten-year average of 51%); the proportion of false-priced favourites to total number of races was just below average (47%, as compared to the ten-year average of 49%); and the proportion of winning false-priced favourites was average (5.5%. compared to 5%). The longest losing run was four selections.

Furthermore, the sprint handicappers, with their strike-rate of 60% (6/10) offset the dearth of repeat 7f winners; and the 66% strike-rate of the same race winners in the early part of the season, usually rather risky propositions, was markedly above the long-term average of 40% winners in this category. In terms of particular performances, MISS ARAGON may have been lucky enough to find another slow race to win (Race 2746 28 July Newmarket).

For the future, the change in the programme offered the possibility of adding another specialist course and distance (Redcar 7f), while the programme added one or two new opportunities at established courses for specialists.

The present trends in racing are likely to increase the number of opportunities available to course and distance winners. I hope that my book has shown you that, with a modicum of effort, you will be able to make good profits from my *Ten Minute System.*